Sandy's Daily Diaries

101 DAYS OF SOCIAL DISTANCING

Sandy Thomson

For Alice

Sandy's Daily Diaries

1

2

∽

Introduction

In March 2020, as the United Kingdom was beginning to feel the full effects of the Covid-19 pandemic, I began to write a daily diary on social media, just for the amusement of family and friends. During social distancing, followed by a full lockdown, I recorded my everyday events and activities and tried to see the funny side of daily life.

No-one was more surprised than I when, within a few days, my diary entries had become so popular I had amassed more than a thousand followers worldwide.

Thanks to the encouragement of all those followers, plus my family and close friends, I managed to keep writing for a hundred and one consecutive days, and I've been encouraged to share my diaries with a wider audience by publishing them in a book. So, at last, here it is!

This is a book for everyone. Nothing controversial, nothing offensive and nothing political, just gentle humour all the way through. You can share it with your five year old child or your ninety five year old granny.

These diaries are simply a record of how a pensioner in the north of Scotland spent his days in social isolation, and my aim was to try to find a little humour in every activity and event. They made thousands of people smile during a very difficult time, and whether you've already read them on social media, or whether you're discovering them here for the first time, I hope they make you smile today.

Sandy Thomson
November 2020

3

*

4

~

Social Distancing Diary – Day 1, a day of cancellations
Monday 16th March 2020
And so it begins.....
Should have been in school today supervising an exam but had to ask a colleague to step in. School is a dangerous environment, no-one coughs like a kid who wants to be sent home.

Had a long morning walk in the woods on a crisp frosty morning. Met my neighbour, had a loud chat across a three-metre exclusion zone.

Returned theatre tickets for a show which I was really looking forward to.

Cancelled dinner reservation with colleagues which I was really looking forward to.

Deep joy, Council Tax statement arrived - £6 per month increase so could be worse I suppose.

Very happy to learn that my friends have made it home to Conon Bridge, from Barcelona. How will they know the difference? Conon Bridge is just like Barcelona but with slightly more wine.

They're in isolation but at least they're home, and together.

Had a short teatime walk with M when she came home from work. We're due to visit M Junior this weekend, will review later in the week.

There are rumours of a possible "lockdown" situation. Fingers crossed it doesn't happen, or at least before we get to visit.

Popmaster score: Round 1 – 3 points Round 2 – 3 points.

5

❦

Social Distancing Diary – Day 2, a day of disappointments. And a dream ring.

Long morning walk in the woods, sunshine and showers. Met a local collie dog but didn't allow him to breathe on me.

Cancelled weekly attendance at my lovely volunteering job with local charity. Will miss it terribly.

My elderly neighbour has come home following a seven week stay in hospital. I've had to explain why she can't have a hug.

Noted - the Grand National has been cancelled. This will save me a considerable amount of money.

Noted - the Gathering Music Festival has been cancelled. This will save me a considerable amount of liver damage.

Still awaiting a decision on the Chelsea Flower Show, which M and I have tickets for. *[Breaking News – it's cancelled too. M is devastated, she had such plans for Monty Don.]*

M Junior texted to say she and bump are officially self-isolating, in line with advice from her employer. We're still planning to see her this weekend.

Very wet afternoon so no walkies. Caught up with a couple of episodes of "Babylon Berlin", very intriguing TV drama, set just after WW1 and before Hitler's rise to power. German with subtitles, reminds me of my only (but very useful) German phrase - "*pomfritz und bier bitte*"

Had online chat with a fellow Chief Invigilator from another school. She's as worried about the exams as I am, loads of Invigilators are elderly (sorry, I mean mature) and we'll struggle to staff the exams. Come on SQA, make a decision.

M came home and regaled me with some tales of what happened in her school. Unfortunately most of them involve bodily functions so can't be repeated here. On the plus side, she did bring me a Harry Gow's dream ring.

Ended the day with Joanna Lumley in the Caribbean. Only on telly, sadly.

Popmaster score: Round 1 – 15 points Round 2 – 3 points

6

⌢

Social Distancing Diary – Day 3, a day of culinary achievement

Now that I'm settling into my "social distancing", M is taking great delight in describing me to everyone as a "social outcast". In her own mind, she's convinced this is funny.

Popped into Tesco this morning for bread and milk, took a deep breath before entering but actually it wasn't very busy. Fascinating to see how (most) customers try to keep the mandatory 2-metre exclusion zone around ourselves. Literally swerving to avoid each other, like some geriatric Latin American dancing display team. Or like our brave RAF lads steering these nasty Russian intruders away from our airspace.

Oops did I say that out loud? Sorry Vlad, please don't send the boys round. We're all comrades now, nyet?

It's hard to judge how far 2 metres is, perhaps I should start carrying a broom handle. M Junior's partner is a farmer, maybe he'd lend me a cattle prod. That would keep the queues moving too.

Topped up the car with fuel for the weekend trip. Used the "pay at pump" option to avoid having to go into the shop. Carried out the whole transaction whilst wearing my driving gloves, tapping in the PIN was interesting but I only had to do it twice.

At last, decision announced by ScotGov – Scottish schools will close on Friday, probably until after the summer holidays. I feel sorry for my local school, Dingwall Academy, whose motto, somewhat unfortunately, is "salve corona". Well would you send your kid to a school with the word "corona" above the door?

As the SQA's Chief Invigilator in a large secondary school, I'm naturally worried about how, or even whether, the exams will run. More news coming tomorrow, apparently. Meantime I hear Boris has cancelled GCSEs in England.

Here's the culinary bit: Inspired by BBC's "Masterchef", got busy in the kitchen. Using my newly-bought milk, made a pudding for tonight. Ok so it's only a Bird's Trifle but still counts as cooking. You have to stir it and everything.

It was a sunny afternoon (who remembers lazing, like the Kinks?) so as well as a morning walk I had an afternoon one. The downside is that I only had time for one episode of Babylon Berlin so only one new word added to my German vocabulary since yesterday: "tot" which means "dead". Sadly, many of the characters from episode 1 are already "tot" and I'm only at episode 6.

No Joanna on telly tonight. Is there no justice?

7

Social Distancing Diary – Day 4, a day of refunds. Or perhaps not.

Frosty start, then heavy rain, then sunshine. Usual walk round woods 7am, anti-clockwise today for a change. Encountered the same dogs as yesterday, but in a different direction.

Bin lorry came this morning, which is about as exciting as it gets around here. The only way I know which bin to put out on which day is to observe my neighbour's selection and copy him. I don't know how he keeps track, he's a retired teacher so maybe he keeps a register or something.

Thursday is my housework day, did all the hoovering, dusting, surfaces and floors. The house is gleaming and smells delightful. There's a theory that I spray Mr Sheen in the air, and liberally dowse the loo with toilet duck just before M comes home. Of course I deny it. Wouldn't you?

Tonight we should have been in Eden Court Theatre watching "Hello Dolly" but since the theatre is closed we're stuck with a night at home with the telly. On the plus side, a charming girl from Eden Court phoned this morning and asked me whether I'd like a refund. She said later that it was the first time she'd had her hand bitten off over the phone.

Also, the Royal Horticultural Society emailed to tell me that my refund for the abandoned Chelsea Flower Show is being processed. This will soften the blow for M, who is still lamenting the loss of her chance to lay hands upon Monty Don. Mr Don remains happily ignorant of his escape.

Alas, EasyJet aren't so forthcoming with the refunds. They're offering me alternative flights, but definitely no money back. I'm tempted to fly to somewhere I don't like, just to annoy them.

Now that we no longer have a dog we've started receiving visits from a stray cat who sneaks into the garden and eats the bread M puts out for the birds. We've called him El Gato, which just goes to show that these Spanish night classes were a good investment.

M is very protective of her garden birds. She's constantly on patrol, fending off crows and seagulls with a combination of shouting, arm waving and throwing satsumas. Now El Gato has come on the scene I expect he'll get a share of this soft fruit bombardment.

My worries about the exams are over. Scot Gov is taking a leaf out of Boris's book and has cancelled the entire exam diet. I've had to break the news to my 20-strong team of invigilators that they're going to miss out on their (admittedly meagre) salary this summer. I will miss the buzz of the exams, and the money of course.

Due to the SQA excitement and having to dash to the Post Office to send 20 letters, no time for Babylon Berlin today. Also, another night of telly without the fragrant Ms Lumley. Come on, BBC.

Popmaster score: Round 1 – 9 points Round 2 – 15 points.

8

∾

Social Distancing Diary – Day 5, a day of winnings. And a dogfight.

Happy news – I'm officially a lottery winner! Deep joy, until I realised that the prize for matching two numbers in the Scottish Children's Lottery is a mere free entry for Monday's draw. Keep your fingers crossed for me, chums.

Friday morning – I should have been at my volunteer job in Highland Hospice, counting cash in the Finance Office. It's always interesting to see the kind of things people put in collection tins. Foreign coins, steel washers and these wee blue plastic Tesco tokens are very common. I wish someone would invent a device to say "unexpected item in the coin machine", in an annoying Asda checkout voice.

Apparently the most valuable British coin is the 1917 George V Gold Sovereign. Surprisingly, no one has thus far put one of those in the charity box.

Friday evening – I should have been out to dinner in Inverness with some special friends, was looking forward to a good night out and a catch up, but yet again I have to settle for a night in. [Breaking news – Boris has announced closure of pubs and restaurants so it looks like no-one else is getting a night out either]

A cold start to the day, with my morning walk livened up by a couple of dogs having a disagreement. It started off with some innocent bottom sniffing but quickly escalated into fang-baring aggression. Reminiscent of the end of term school disco back in the day. Luckily the owners soon intervened so I didn't have to risk rabies.

Lovely sunny morning. M put a washing on before she left for school and I hung it out after my traumatic walk. Carefully sorted everything out so that smallest things could go on the left, largest on the right. My underwear fits in naturally between "beach towel" and "bell tent".

Had a second walk again today, and another shouty 3-metre distance conversation with one of the neighbours. Social distancing, mutual deafness and traffic noise makes communication difficult but as he said, we mustn't take anything for granite.

Won't be going away after all this weekend. We've decided not to travel until it becomes safe to do so again. Disappointed not to be seeing M Junior, Farmer J and Dog F but still 15 weeks to go until Bump emerges so hope we'll get together before then.

Meantime M Junior tells me there's a thing called WhatsApp video chat (or something) so we'll be having a go at that. I'm not too optimistic about mastering such modern technological wizardry, I'm only now beginning to get the hang of the ballpoint pen.

Speaking of ballpoint pens, I forgot to tell you M brought home a copy of The Times yesterday. I started the crossword after tea and finished it at 2.30 today, a remarkable 20 hours. OK I say finished, but I may have "invented" some of the answers. Remember Bart Simpson's scrabble word "quijibo"? Fits nicely at 12 across.

M brought home an electric pencil sharpener from her school, in the hope that I can fix it. She thinks there's something jammed inside it, possibly a finger belonging to a small child. Surely Mummy would have noticed if little Johnny came home missing a finger.

Anyway, with some trepidation I dismantled it and was relieved to find, jammed in the bowels of the machine, not a detached 8-year-old finger but a piece of broken wax crayon. Removed the obstruction, reassembled the device and sharpened every pencil in the house to a fine point. Must remember not to plunge my hand blindly into the kitchen drawer for fear of impalement.

Tomorrow is Saturday, M doesn't work weekends so we'll be together for two days. Hope we don't fall out but if we do you'll be first to know.

Popmaster score: Round 1 – 9 points Round 2 – 9 points.

9

~

Social Distancing Diary – Day 6, a day of walking. And more walking.

No work for M today so we had a leisurely start, ie a lie-in until 7am.

As soon as we were up M sprang into action, stripping the bed sheets and putting on a wash because it was a nice sunny morning. My personal belief, not shared by M, is that bed sheets need changed only once or twice a year. Same applies to underpants – wear for a month, wear inside out for a month, commando for a month, job done.

In extreme conditions you can swap with your neighbour for a further month but I'm not convinced the 80-year-old Italian lady next door would be entirely comfortable with the concept. Mamma mia!

Our usual Saturday routine consists of a trip to Inverness, a cooked breakfast in town and a couple of hours shopping. Today, of course, there's no chance of any sausage, bacon and egg so had to content myself with a bowl of microwaved porridge at home. Remember the TV adverts for breakfast oats where the kids appeared to glow in the dark? My nuclear porridge has the same effect.

To minimise my exposure to crowds, we decided to shop independently this morning. M drove to Inverness for grocery shopping, while I walked to Dingwall to buy a top-up for our electric meter. It's one of those pre-paid ones where you get your token topped up in the shop then come home and insert it in the meter and voila! Your meter is topped up! Unfortunately, because technology and I are often in conflict, it doesn't always work.

When that happens I have to phone the electric company's helpline which appears to be based somewhere east of Delhi, and while the operators are always polite and helpful there are inevitable language difficulties. Their English is better than mine but their Gaelic is sadly lacking.

Because there's a danger of infection from handling cash, I'm trying to pay for everything using my contactless card, which is very advanced technology for me. In fact I have trouble remembering the term "contactless", often referring to it as "cordless" or "cashless", much to M's annoyance. She was most embarrassed one day when I asked the young lady barista in Starbucks if I could pay "topless".

M came home from Inverness with almost everything on the shopping list. We're not doing panic buying because there's only two of us and we could easily survive for a couple of weeks on the food we have in the freezer and in the kitchen cupboards. I'm sure that, right at the back, there are tins of food which were canned during the war. And I don't mean the Gulf War, or the Falklands War.

She brought me my favourite Saturday newspaper, the Scotsman. I do the prize crossword every week, so far without success. But in their sister publication, Scotland on Sunday, I once won the crossword and then began entering it in M Junior's name. She also won it and just for fun I began entering in the name of our rabbit at the time, whose name was Basil. And so, inevitably, it came to pass that in the following week's paper the crossword winner was announced as "Basil Thomson from Dingwall".

Following my successful completion of the crossword, M and I walked (again for me!) to Dingwall to pop it into the mail. It's around a mile and a half each way and I did it twice, so that makes my daily walking total at least 6 miles. And all those calories expended without a cooked breakfast. No wonder I'm fading away.

No Popmaster score today, it isn't on at weekends. I'm considering returning my wireless licence.

10

〜

Social Distancing Diary – Day 7, a day of wartime memories

Sundays are traditionally very quiet here, almost to the point of being boring. Pretty much like Mondays, Tuesdays, Wednesdays and all the other days.

Hoorah! It's Mother's Day in Socially Distanced Britain. We've all been warned not to go and visit our mothers or grandmothers because they're vulnerable, but there are ways and means. M Junior cleverly sent me an email yesterday, with an instruction to follow the link in it and print the resulting document. In secret. Amazingly I succeeded in this task and lo and behold! A Mother's Day voucher for M, which I gave her this morning. So that, combined with the wonder that is WhatsApp, allowed mother and daughter to have contact on the day.

This virus better be gone by Father's Day. I expect more than a long-distance voucher when it's my turn. At the very least, a visit to McDonald's.

My own mother played a vital part in WW2 by serving with

the Royal Air Force. She was one of those girls you see in old war movies using long sticks to push model aircraft around a big table-top map, while the dashing young RAF officer on the radio shouts "bandits in sector three" and "let 'em 'ave it, Biffo", and other inspiring exclamations.

She and her colleagues were in the WAAF, which actually stands for "Women's Auxiliary Air Force", but some of the more red-blooded young pilots seemed to think it stood for "Women Are Always Free". And since most of these young men were bristling with testosterone, you can imagine how the mighty Luftwaffe wasn't the only threat facing these girls.

Luckily, my mother escaped both Hitler's bombs and the attentions of her over-eager male colleagues, otherwise I might have had a Brylcreem-anointed father and be writing this from a disused airfield in rural Norfolk.

Incidentally, a father anointed with Brylcreem isn't the same as a father who's well oiled. Although that title can sometimes be applied to me.

Anyway, I'd better tell you something about my day. Sunday lie-in, same as Saturday, 7am. No washing today for a change, so a walk round the woods with M before breakfast. Met two dogs – one of the fighters from the other day, and one new one who looked slightly aggressive, but when I bravely pushed M to the front he soon backed down.

Then M walked to the shop for the Sunday papers. I had my usual nuclear porridge while keeping the garden free from marauding seagulls and crows. No sign of El Gato today, I wonder if he's self isolating.

I failed to finish the Scotland on Sunday crossword today, and have become quite sad. M said I mustn't get "too down" about it then she began laughing at some joke only she understands. Don't know what's so funny about that, it's five across I'm stuck with.

Sunday dinner – chicken casserole, followed by strawberry jelly, followed by yet another walk around the woods with M. She seems determined to keep me fit, or wear me into the ground, I'm not sure which. She's back to work tomorrow, so I can have a quieter day, and an illicit snooze on the sofa before she comes home.

11

∾

Social Distancing Diary – Day 8, a day of DIY avoidance

Oh well, it looks like we're in lockdown after all. It's many years since I've been grounded but Boris has managed it.

Nicola has ordered all shops in Scotland to close down, apart from food shops, pharmacies and other essentials. I will especially miss browsing in B & Q (Other DIY shops are available, but not right now). I can spend hours staring knowingly and nodding manfully at the range of tools. And pretending I know what they're all for.

Ken Bruce is presenting his BBC Radio 2 show from his home. Luckily he's still able to include all his usual features. Mornings without Popmaster would be pretty empty.

M was at work so I was able to have just the one walk today. It was a nice one, third dry day in a row so no mud to wade through. Luckily the path through our local woods is quite wide, and the verges are dry, so when people meet they can observe the recommended 2-metre gap.

Dogs, however, don't seem to have grasped the concept of

distancing. All the local ones know that I always have a supply of doggy treats in my pocket, and they invade my personal space without any hesitation. But who can refuse a pair of big sad (hungry) eyes?

My horoscope in today's newspaper reads: "a chance to connect with a friend and enjoy spending time together". Also refers to my "...part in a group project". Hmmm I don't know who the astrologer is but she's way off the mark with that one. Maybe she was looking through the wrong end of her telescope.

Worryingly, M has unearthed her stock of decorating materials, ie paint, wallpaper etc which she bought last summer in the faint hope that I might paint the hall and paper the bathroom. I had put the job off until the October holidays, then put it off again until Christmas. It was definitely in my long term plan for Easter but now that M has been forced to stop work there's a good chance she'll get fed up waiting, and tackle both jobs herself.

Of course I won't just stand back and let her do it alone, oh no. I'm always on hand to give advice, like: "you missed a bit", "that doesn't match", and my favourite: "what time's dinner". That's usually the point at which I get sent to the naughty step, ie my shed. Where I consider the error of my ways, with only my portable radio and secret stash of beer for company.

Finally finished the Scotland on Sunday crossword at lunchtime on Monday. It was a real stinker this week. Are crosswords getting harder, or is my brain getting weaker? I think we all know the answer to that.

Popmaster score: Round 1 – 9 points Round 2 – 6 points.

12

∽

Social Distancing Diary – Day 9, a day of sore feet

First day of lockdown. M popped into school for an hour to make sure everything was secure, that the heating was set properly and the bins emptied. Then that was the building abandoned until further notice. On the way home she called into the local shop for milk and bought me a copy of The Times, in the hope that the crossword will keep me quiet for a while. Last time, it kept me quiet for almost 24 hours so she considers it money well spent.

Boris says we can go out for one period of exercise per day. We feel safe enough to have two walks a day, because we live in a quiet area and have immediate access to the great outdoors. For our afternoon walk I made a big mistake by allowing M to choose the route. Off we set after lunch, for what I hoped would be a gentle half-hour stroll. Two hours and 6 miles later we got home.

And the last three miles were on tarred roads. Oh my poor feet. I don't suppose the shoe shops are still open. At this rate

I'll be going through a pair of boots every two weeks. The good news is that tomorrow I get to choose where we go. Perhaps I'll take my bike, that'll teach her.

Nice dry day again, with a strong wind. At last the garden is beginning to dry out after being flooded for most of the winter. I'm hoping to make a start on digging the veg patch this week, if I can find the spade in the black hole that is the garden shed. Over the winter anything that needs to be disposed of or hidden gets chucked into the shed so when spring arrives it resembles a dumping ground. Like a teenager's bedroom but with plant pots, and fewer dirty dishes.

According to the newspaper, we were all due to receive a text message from the UK Government advising us about precautions during the lockdown period. M got hers this morning, but no sign of mine. I was beginning to despair that Boris had forgotten me, or worse, was ignoring me. I was just about to dash off a strongly worded letter to Downing Street when it arrived, at last, this evening. Lucky escape Boris, you wouldn't like a letter from Mr Angry.

Also, M has had a text message from our local GP practice advising her about procedures for contacting them during the current emergency. I received no such text so obviously the NHS has classified me as "expendable". Imagine not being worth even the cost of a text message.

I've finally got around to watching the last episode of Babylon Berlin. Without giving away any spoilers, I have to report that I'm still confused about who is who, and on which side, and where from. All I can say with certainty is that they spent the entire series shooting, stabbing and blowing each other up. And the men were just as bad.

And finally, I'm happy to report that, at last, the DFS Sale is over.

Popmaster score: Round 1 – 15 points Round 2 – 3 points.

13

~~~

Social Distancing Diary – Day 10, a day of DIH (Do It Herself)

No gardening today after all. Awoke to heavy rain, which has obviously been falling most of the night so my nicely drying garden is soaked again. Oh dear what a shame, I'll just need to resign myself to spending the day relaxing with yesterday's Times crossword.

M and I both believe that in this difficult time of lockdown it's important to keep our daily routines as near to normal as possible. Which suits me because it means she gets up at 6am and brings me a cup of tea in bed. The only difference is that instead of going to work she goes for an early morning walk and returns via the local shop for the papers and today – joy of joys – a Harry Gow's dream ring!

I then rise at 7 as usual, have my morning walk at a sensible pace, ie slow with frequent rests, followed by breakfast, followed by settling down with the papers while waiting for Popmaster.

As predicted, the decorating has commenced. During my

post-breakfast newspaper routine I became aware of the sound of some kind of activity in the hall. Eventually it got so loud, and began to be accompanied by scraping noises, I felt obliged to get off my armchair and investigate. There I found M taking all the pictures off the walls and the books off the bookshelves in preparation for the much-anticipated painting. See, I knew that if I delayed it long enough she'd eventually start it herself.

I did lend a hand though. The bookshelves needed to be dismantled and stored in another room and since I'm the only one in the family with O'Grade Woodwork (1967) I was the obvious choice for the job. Boy, I'm good at dismantling things. Putting them back up afterwards will be a different matter, however. That will require planning, which is a thing that all men know how to do, and which can't be rushed, and which M just doesn't appreciate the importance of.

First there's the pre-planning phase, which can't begin until after the painting has been done (and fully dried). Then comes the actual planning phase which includes listing materials required and might necessitate a visit to B & Q for tools. Sadly because of lockdown this can't happen for a few weeks so all the books need to remain strewn on the floor meantime. Sorry dear, these things just can't be rushed.

Incidentally, while I was spending three years in school learning the noble art of woodwork, M was wasting her time studying Latin. She occasionally uses it to speak to me in terms of endearment. One of her favourite pet names for me is *dorkusmalorkus*. I don't know exactly what it means, but isn't it just lovely?

Afternoon walk was my choice today so I chose Dingwall

and back, just to the outskirts. (Dingwall has outskirts? Who knew?) Around three miles, all on safe footpaths so no sore tootsies today.

Popmaster score: Round 1 – 3 points Round 2 – 0 points.

14

෴

Social Distancing Diary – Day 11, a day of not touching ANYTHING

M Junior phoned first thing. She has an Argos voucher to use up before the end of the month and wanted advice about what she should include in her online order, in preparation for baby coming in July. Luckily M beat me to the phone and made sensible suggestions about changing mats, moses baskets, etc. My recommendations would have included a train set, a snooker table and a dartboard.

Immediately after breakfast M launched into her hallway painting again, and she sounded so industrious that my conscience wouldn't allow me to relax so I headed outside in an attempt to look busy. Tried sticking an experimental fork into what's going to be the ultimate veg garden, but it's still too soggy even to stand on. Hope it dries up soon, my seed potatoes have been resting in the spare bedroom for a couple of weeks and are desperate to be planted out.

They've sprouted so well that the room has begun to resemble the steamy jungles of Borneo. I'm sure I hear orangutan noises in the night. M agrees, but says she's already endured more than 30 years of orangutan noises in the bedroom so one or two more won't make any difference.

Having abandoned the digging, I turned my attention to another project. Our Christmas present from Farmer J was a garden centre gift voucher, which we used to purchase a mini greenhouse. Of course it came flat packed and carried a label with the legend of doom: "Some assembly required".

As it turned out, it wasn't as difficult as I had anticipated. Once I worked out how to "connect the top section of Part A to the corresponding side of Part E using Bolt H and tighten using Screws N" it all fell into place nicely. Apart from the roof somehow appearing where I thought the floor should be. And the fact that the doors don't actually open. But that won't matter, indeed it will keep the wee plants nice and cosy inside at all times.

Regular readers will be aware of the importance of the Popmaster radio quiz in my daily routine. Every morning at 10.30 everything – and I mean everything – has to stop for 20 minutes or so. Imagine my consternation when, at 10.24 today, the phone rang! Turned out to be my favourite SQA Co-ordinator with a query about exam materials. She's very efficient at what she does, but her timing needs a little attention. "Room for improvement", as my school report might have stated. Well, did state. Regularly.

Yesterday's clearing of the bookshelves yielding some interesting results. Our bookshelf is rather like an indoor version of the shed from hell – it's where anything gets put that isn't of any use, but might be needed "sometime". Amongst the publications found were the instructions and 12-month warranty for the fridge/freezer we bought in 2008, and the vacuum cleaner from the same year. Also the handbook for an Indesit washing machine, which was the one **before** the one **before** the current one, and which went to washing machine heaven at least 20 years ago.

In addition, there were various ancient theatre programmes, seed catalogues and my old school atlas. "The New Comparative Atlas", published by Oliver and Boyd 1964. If anyone doing a quiz ever needs to know the locations of Yugoslavia, Persia or Siam I have all the answers.

Had my afternoon walk on my own today - painting was in progress and M was determined to finish the hall before going for her own walk. After finishing, she left me alone with clear instructions ringing in my head: "Don't touch ANYTHING!". She's even jammed a stepladder against the living room door to stop me entering the hall from that direction.

Popmaster score: Round 1 – 6 points Round 2 – 18 points.

15

~

Social Distancing Diary – Day 11, a day of order and tidiness

Morning walk was punctuated by the noise of woodpeckers in, well, the woods. I often hear one, but today there were two, hammering like pneumatic drills. Obviously trying to send messages to each other. Using an application called treemail? Unlike dogs, especially boy dogs, who use weemail.

M decided to do her weekly shopping today, instead of the usual Saturday, on the principle that it might be less busy. Sadly, I'm not allowed to go because of my so-called "underlying health issues" (thanks, Chief Medical Officer) so she set off to Dingwall alone. The queue to get access to Tesco was so long, she gave up and did her shopping elsewhere, and was lucky enough to get almost everything on the list, with the notable exception of toilet rolls (which is ok because we have an inexhaustible supply of unfinished Times crosswords).

Luckily she was able to get a couple of bottles of beer, so that's Friday night sorted.

The hallway painting is complete, dried and – so far at least – unmarked by greasy fingerprints. Next job for the O'Grade Woodwork graduate – refitting the bookshelves. Because of the current crisis I was persuaded to skip the usual pre-planning, planning and pondering stages and just get on with it. So, three sets of shelf supports installed, and three perfectly fitted shelves. Minimum of swearing, no serious injuries and very nearly level. That's what I call a result.

Then, of course, all the books, pamphlets, leaflets and other publications which had spent the last few days on the spare bed-room floor had to be reinstalled on the shelves. But not without some serious weeding out. We've filled two boxes of books for the charity shops when they reopen, and our paper recycling bin, which only got emptied yesterday, is bulging with all the out-of-date printed matter which had gathered and multiplied over the past 20 years.

So now our book area is a shining example of order and tidiness. We have a travel section (atlases, road maps); a culture section (music, poetry, literature); a reference section (including the dictionary which was Basil Bunny's crossword prize) and one copy of "How to be a Good Husband", published in 1983. And unopened.

The hall is now a clean, delicate shade of white. Polished Pebble, I think the paint manufacturer calls it, but it looks white to me. Therefore we have christened it "Whitehall". Next on the list is the "Throne Room". You can guess what that is.

I've been informed that during the Throne Room redecoration there will be restricted access to the facilities, with a rota system in place. My appointed slot, apparently, is 10.30am – 10.40am on weekdays. I appealed to the management for a different allocation on the grounds that 10.30 is my dedicated popmaster time but my appeal was rejected with the statement "popmaster or poopmaster, the choice is yours". Harsh.

Tomorrow is Saturday, the weekend. Don't expect it will feel any different to any other day. Stay well, my friends, in these strange times.

Popmaster score: Round 1 – 18 points Round 2 – 9 points.

16

〰

Social Distancing Diary – Day 13, a day of wondering what happened to Day 12

The more observant amongst you will have noticed that the day before yesterday (Thursday) was Day 11, and yesterday (Friday) was also Day 11. Most of you were kind enough to spare my feelings and refrain from pointing this out.

Today is Saturday, March 28 if you must know, and with it comes the weekly ritual of changing the bedding, washing it and hanging it out. Not for long today though. First it rained, then hailed and then finally snowed so we rushed out and bundled the washing into the tumble dryer. Ten minutes later the snow stopped and the sun came out again, so we reversed the process.

This time it took half an hour for the snow/hail to start again so this time the washing was stuffed into the tumble dryer permanently. There are limits to the amount of rushing I can do on Saturdays. Especially without my traditional Morrison's breakfast inside me.

Still no sign of El Gato, but we've inherited a whole new set of visitors. A few days ago we awoke to a small brown lady duck in the garden, being wooed by a vigorous-looking shiny green male mallard. Next day, the same lady duck was there, but this time with two male attendants. She's obviously a lady of very dubious morals because this morning there she was again, with no fewer than FOUR green feathered (and very ardent) gentlemen pursuing her.

She teases them by flitting from garden to garden, and they follow her faithfully, each hoping to be daddy to her babies. According to the RSPB a mallard lays between 8 and 13 eggs each time, so she'd probably appreciate four husbands to help after hatching time.

For our fitness activity this afternoon we walked to Dingwall. M needed to get a top-up for the electric meter so we combined that errand with our daily exercise. I waited outside while she went into the shop, and I had a look along the high street. The street was deserted, it was like standing at the South Pole, but marginally colder. And with slightly fewer penguins.

Had a telephone call from my chum, who got back from Barcelona a couple of weeks ago. He has been very unlucky, his Barcelona quarantine expired on Monday, just in time for Boris to impose the lockdown. Very bad timing but at least he got about three hours of freedom. Which is more than they get in Barlinnie.

Anyway, being a retired bank manager he has a good insight into the financial aspect of the current crisis, and thanks to his advice I have now frozen my Sky Sports subscription. To be honest I was dreading having a conversation with Sky's helpline operator in New Delhi. My inability to understand simple questions, and encroaching deafness, usually make negotiations difficult but I'm happy (and surprised) to report that it was a really easy process so we're now Sky-Sports-free until the world of sport comes alive again. No point paying for something that's no use to you, as the Queen might have said when she cancelled Prince Harry's annual allowance.

M is a huge football fan and is missing her sport terribly. On Saturday afternoons she displays classic withdrawal symptoms, pacing around, sighing loudly and muttering in a strange language which only she understands: "...Mourhino...Guardiola...Klopp...".

My own favourite sport is motorbike racing, and my Sunday afternoons are usually spent in front of the telly with MotoGP and beer, or World Superbikes and beer, or British Superbikes and beer. Now all I have is repeats of The Great Escape. Thank goodness for beer.

No Popmaster today, but if there had been I would have scored 39.

17

∾

Social Distancing Diary – Day 14, a day of daylight saving (yawn)

At 2am this morning the clocks went forward in the UK. I put mine forward to August but when I awoke it was still March and we were still in lockdown.

I went round the house at bedtime last night putting all the clocks forward. I couldn't put my alarm clock forward because I threw it out of the window at 6am one morning in October and haven't seen it since.

No decorating today. I persuaded M to have a day of rest. Except for cooking my Sunday lunch of course. Tomorrow however, the throne room will be getting the treatment. I will be expected to remove the bathroom heater from its mountings on the wall. Fine, except I haven't a clue how I fitted it to the wall in the first place, all these years ago.

I'm lucky to have many musical friends, and some of them have been giving concerts online, from their homes. It takes a lot of courage to sing and play live, and also to expose your wallpaper and choice of curtains to the critical gaze of the watching world. And there's always the risk of being upstaged by your adorable dog/ beautiful cat/ cute kids.

I usually attend a series of traditional music festivals throughout the year, but of course all of them have been cancelled, at least up until August, so it's nice to be able to see and hear my friends via Facebook Live. This is a difficult year for musicians. I've only got one booking still valid this year, for a ceilidh in Laggan on 1st August, but I'm not optimistic about it going ahead.

I did consider giving an online concert myself but then I thought: the nation is having a hard enough time already so it would be a shame to increase your misery.

This afternoon it was dry, so M and I did our 6-mile circuit walk. M says she feels the walk is getting shorter. I don't agree, I believe it's my legs which are getting shorter. To make it a little easier I've started using a walking stick, which M is taking delight in describing as my "pensioner's pole".

I've been troubled by a weak ankle. I first felt it last November, when I was invigilating Prelim exams and found it painful walking upstairs to the exam room. My GP says it's due to a combination of getting older and carrying a little too much weight. OK, she didn't actually use the word "little".

I blame my Chief Invigilator basic training, which is very similar to Army basic training but with added aggression. In lesson 1 the key word was drummed into us: "supervise, supervise, supervise". Unfortunately I was sitting right at the back, slightly deaf and not really paying attention, so I thought the trainer said "soup and pies". Therefore I saw it as my duty to indulge in both, in large quantities.

Beware! Big brother is watching everything you do on the internet. A few days ago, in this diary, I mentioned that I had passed my O'Grade Woodwork exam in 1967. Yesterday, to my great surprise, I got a message inviting me to join the Woodworkers Guild of America. When I investigated their website I found that the projects on offer include something called a "toilet paper stand". Might be OK in America, but here in shortage-ridden Britain it would simply be a "stand".

Incidentally, now that we're not allowed to drive, the price of petrol is the lowest it's been for years. And just to annoy us, Highland Council have announced all car parks are free until further notice.

Finally, I hear on the news that we're all going to get a letter from Boris about covid-19. Hope he doesn't lick the envelope.

Popmaster tomorrow. Please don't phone me at 10.30.

18

~

Social Distancing Diary – Day 15, a day of gratitude. And a wee froggy.

I don't believe it! Two weeks ago today I began this diary, purely as a bit of fun for family and friends, and now here I am with more than 1400 online followers. I'm overwhelmed and surprised, but very touched that so many of you seem to enjoy my daily stories from my very ordinary life. Thank you for your feedback and funny comments, keep them coming! And please share with your friends.

More importantly, I began inviting donations for my chosen charity, the Highland Hospice, with an ambitious target of £999. Today, I see that we've passed that target and now sitting at more than £1,000 so thank you all for your generosity and, if you haven't had the chance to donate yet, please do so, even £1 from everyone will be a significant boost to the Hospice at this difficult time.

Anyway, what happened today?

M is still in decorating mode, and having avoided the job

since Friday, the removal of the bathroom heater could wait no longer. The installation instructions had been lost many years ago, along with my memory of how I fitted it to the wall in the first place. I did do some secret fiddling around at the weekend but was still none the wiser. However, help is always at hand. As usual on a weekday, M was up at 6am and off out for her morning walk. As soon as I heard the door slam I leapt out of bed, switched on the computer and googled "Dimplex bathroom heater installation". And there it was – all the instructions and diagrams I could possibly need. A quick print then back to bed to memorise the procedure and act all innocent when M came home.

After breakfast, the inevitable question was raised. She enquired, with doubt in her voice, as to when I might be able to remove the heater, and did I know how to do it anyway? "Of course I do", I declared. "Trust me, I know how to do all these manly things". I then proceeded to remove it from the wall swiftly and efficiently without any fuss or bad language, much to her surprise. Thanks Mr Google, you saved the day!

At last a start has been made on the vegetable garden. After Popmaster I manfully marched out, fully kitted out with everything a serious gardener needs – boots, spade, mug of tea, loud radio to attract the neighbours' attention so that they can be impressed by how industrious I am. Soil is still quite heavy so it rapidly became tiring and after digging three rows my prayers were answered – it began to rain. Result - immediate retreat to the shed, where the illicit beer stash lives, and a happy half hour spent with BBC Radio 2 before heading into the house shaking my head and grumbling about my gardening being interrupted.

During my afternoon walk I was alerted by a concerned and caring neighbour about a small frog who was attempting to cross the road not too far away. She was worried he would be flattened by a passing motorist and, if it hadn't been for lockdown and Boris's restrictions on driving, he surely would have been. When I reached the place there he was, hopping manfully (or should that be frogfully?) across the road towards our neighbouring farmer's field. What he evidently hadn't realised was that when he did make it across the road, he was about to be faced with a stone wall barring him from entry.

As anyone knows, a two-inch frog can't possibly jump a four foot wall so I did my good deed for the day, carried him across the road, lifted him up and placed him on top of the wall, facing into the field. Just then I realised I hadn't kept two metres away from him, so I hope he doesn't have the virus. Although it's probably safe enough. He was wearing a mask.

Popmaster score: Round 1 – 12 points Round 2 – 12 points.

19

༄

Social Distancing Diary – Day 16, a day of weary muscles
On my morning walk I pass close to the main Inverness-Ullapool road. I'm always impressed by the number of delivery lorries heading to Ullapool to catch the ferry to Stornoway, and keep the good folks of the Western Isles supplied with groceries. The islanders were hopeful that their isolation from the mainland would protect them from the virus, but I was sad to hear that a couple of cases have now been diagnosed on Lewis. The islander's usual response in times of trouble is to have a ceilidh but sadly they can't even do that now.

In normal times island life looks like this: Ferry broken down? Have a ceilidh! Stock market crashed? Have a ceilidh! Russians invading? Have a ceilidh! But I bet there'll be a monster ceilidh when this is all over. I wish them well, and hope I get invited.

Further to yesterday's frog experience, I fear isolation is finally having an effect on M's mental state. This morning she told me that when she got up she thought she could hear a faint squeaky voice calling for help. And when she went to investigate, she found a wee froggy on top of the wall begging: "Help, help, a horrible man lifted me up here yesterday and I can't get down". Is she making it up, or has she finally cracked?

The wallpapering in the Throne Room has now been completed, along with the painting of the skirting boards. And the heater has been reinstalled, cabinet and toilet roll holder fitted to the wall so now we're "good to go", if you know what I mean.

It's nice to have a different pattern to gaze at whilst "in residence". In normal times, when M is at work, I usually take a paper in there with me and have a nice read to pass the time. However I suspect any rustling sounds through the bathroom door would lead to a serious talking to, perhaps even a ban.

At least she can't divorce me while we're in lockdown. Ha!

Had another couple of sessions in the planned vegetable garden. Got rained off twice but managed to get quite a lot of digging done. Ooh my poor muscles. It's quite a few years since I did any serious digging, so by lunchtime I was very sore and weary, and ready for a wee snooze.

No such luck. Immediately after lunch I settled down hopefully in my armchair with the BBC News, which usually sends me to sleep faster than any sedative, but just as I was dozing off M announced brightly: "Time for walkies!" Poor M, she'd been stuck in the house all morning with her wallpaper and paint, and was desperate to get out. All protestations about sore back, weak ankle, etc were swiftly brushed aside and so off I set, supported by my pensioner's pole.

We seem to have got into a habit of alternating our daily

walks, three miles one day and six miles the next and so on. Today was the six-miler, started dry, but had a heavy shower halfway round. Very pleased to see that lots of people are out walking. Even those who hadn't previously been in the habit of walking are taking advantage of the opportunity. If we can just escape the virus I'm sure the nation's fitness will have improved by the time this lockdown ends.

M junior has been sending us photos of the latest addition to the farm – a small flock of chickens. I think the plan is that when Farmer J is busy with the Big Things (sheep, cattle, John Deere tractors), M Junior and Dog F will take care of the chickens. However, judging by the photos Dog F sees them not as a source of eggs but as a source of amusement, and possible playmates. I hope they can run. Very fast.

Popmaster score: Round 1 – 15 points Round 2 – 0 points.

20

∾

Social Distancing Diary – Day 17, a day of traditions

April Fool's Day! One of my traditions is searching in the papers to spot the inevitable April Fool's Day spoof story. One paper today has Prince Harry shopping in a supermarket in LA, while another reports that Lewis Capaldi has taken up sheep farming. In Lewis of course. Meanwhile the lady I met walking her dog this morning tried to tell me that Lidl has had a delivery of toilet rolls. "Ha ha nice try missus", said I, "I'm not falling for that one".

Imagine how I felt a couple of hours later when the next door neighbour came home from shopping with, yes, a 24-pack of the finest toilet tissue from Germany. Soft, strong and very obedient.

Another tradition M and I have is the immature "pinch, punch, first of the month" nonsense. I say nonsense because I seldom know what day, month or year it is, so I never win. This morning I was very rudely awakened at 6am (yes, 6am!) by a nip on the ear and a punch on the shoulder from a triumphant M, crowing "Pinch, punch, first of the month hahaha I win". And she broke the 2-metre exclusion zone to do it.

Another day, another visiting stray. First thing this morning we spotted a scabby ginger cat lurking at the edge of the lawn, eyeing up the blackbirds having their morning feed. He soon made a very sharp exit, pursued by a flying satsuma.

Every day when I go out to top up the water in the bird baths (we have four!) I retrieve the previous 24 hours' worth of satsumas and bring them in to be reused. A row of them sit inside the kitchen window sill, lined up like cannonballs. And, like cannonballs, they get fired with enough velocity to sink a battleship.

Success! In spite of constant rain interruptions the garden has now finally been dug. To put it into perspective, it's around the size of a postage stamp and it only took three days to complete. M says it's a good job I wasn't digging for victory since the war would be over long before I grew anything. A little harsh, I thought.

All I need now is a couple of dry days for the soil to warm up a little so that I can get the well-sprouted Mutant Seed Potatoes from Hell out of the spare room and into the ground. They've now started lifting the lid off their box all by themselves and creeping determinedly towards the door in an attempt to escape. I hope they'll be as vigorous once they're planted.

I need to order some seeds for this newly-created haven of self-sufficiency. Been searching through the kitchen drawers, and all I've found so far is a packet of beetroot seeds from 2015, which came as a free gift with a gardening magazine.

The shops are closed so the only way to obtain seeds and plants is by mail order. I was distressed to find that my favourite garden supplies company has temporarily stopped accepting on-line orders to allow them to catch up with a backlog. So it looks like it's going to be a diet of potatoes and beetroot this year. Low in calories but high in starch. Thank heavens for elasticated waistbands.

Meanwhile, having painted the hallway and papered the bathroom, M has now turned her attention to the kitchen. This is very worrying because the kitchen is the place where food comes from and I fear there may be interruptions to the supply and demand system. The supply chain in this house needs to be very robust, to keep up with my stomach's demands.

Wet walk this afternoon, quite a slow one. Juggling a pensioner's pole and an umbrella ain't easy, let me tell you.

Popmaster score: Round 1 – 3 points Round 2 – 6 points.

21

∽

Social Distancing Diary – Day 18, a day of four seasons

Today started off windy, with leaves flying, like an autumn day. Then it was summer sunshine, followed by spring with rainy showers. Finally, and this happened in the middle of my morning walk, we were hit by a blast of winter, with fierce snow. The wee man and woman in the weather house are going in and out faster than the toilet rolls in Tesco.

The kitchen decorating goes on apace. Two walls yesterday, with one today and the last one planned for tomorrow. My contribution today was to take down the vertical window blinds, and I managed it in spite of my qualification being in Woodwork, not Metalwork. Anyway, taking things down is usually easy, it's putting them back up afterwards that causes me problems.

And because painting was at a critical stage lunch was delayed. And the soup tasted of paint fumes. Maybe I shouldn't have stirred it with the same stick that M was using.

On Monday it was announced that everyone in the country

is to get a personal letter from the Prime Minister. Today is Thursday and mine hasn't arrived yet. Aggrieved, I phoned Downing Street to complain, and his secretary told me: "We sent Boris to the Post Office on Monday, to buy the stamps, but he hasn't come back yet. It seems there's a long queue and they're only allowing two people in at a time".

I hear that Army Reservists are being called up to help with the current crisis. My own service ended almost thirty years ago so I think it's unlikely I'll get my calling-up papers any time soon. In any case they're looking for specific skills. My main skill was getting myself to the front of the cookhouse queue before anyone else and I suspect that's not exactly what they're looking for.

And for those of you who would accuse me of "part-time", "playtime" and "peacetime" soldiering, might I remind you that it's thanks to me that you were all able to sleep soundly in your beds during the Cold War while I faced the might of the Red Army just across the border. It was hard, let me tell you. I spent many a lonely hour in the 1970s and 80s down a hole in the ground in Central Europe, emerging only occasionally for beer, fresh air, beer, chips and beer.

Away back on Day 4 you will remember I had tried to get money back for our flights to London in May for the Chelsea Flower Show. EasyJet would only offer alternative flights, no refunds. However now that they've grounded all their planes it's possible to get refunds after all. Well that's the theory. In practice it's turned out not to be so simple. I've been phoning their customer services every few minutes (it feels like) for two days now. Sometimes I get an engaged tone, occasionally I get a reassuring voice telling me how busy they are, and to call back later.

I do understand the pressure the airlines are under, and so I'm refraining from writing my usual "strongly worded letter". But M needs compensation, not so much for the flight, but for missing out on meeting her hero Monty Don. I understand how she feels, if I was missing out on a chance to meet the fragrant Ms Lumley I'd be distraught too.

Six mile walk this afternoon, amazingly it remained dry all the way round but very windy. Helped to blow the paint fumes out of my hair anyway.

Popmaster score: Round 1 – 6 points Round 2 – 6 points.

22

∿

Social Distancing Diary – Day 19, a day of blind confusion

Woke up to snow in the garden today, which is nice because it covers up my rough digging of the past few days and makes it look nice and even. Not enough snow to make a snowman though, unless it's a very very small one. Snowbaby, perhaps.

It's Friday already, the weekend starts here but there's no way to tell the difference. M went for her weekly Friday shopping and once again managed to get everything on the list plus a packet of paracetomol, which was a bonus. I don't often admit it, but I do occasionally incur the usual aches and pains associated with getting older, so it's not unknown for me to take a couple of paracetomol now and again. The funny thing is that since covid-19 arrived I haven't felt the need to take any. Which is just as well, because until today we didn't have any.

While she was away, I decided it would be a good time to tackle the reinstallation of the dreaded kitchen vertical blind. I prefer to do these things without an audience. Especially since the blind width is 1455mm and my wingspan is a mere 1450mm. Fitted the hanging brackets, easy. Using the original screw holes, easy. Clipped the top bar of the blind to the brackets, easy. Pulled the rod to close the blinds and – aaargh! The slats began falling out of the end of the top bar and crumpling gently into the sink.

Obviously something was amiss, and indeed it was. Removal of the top bar revealed an open end – surely there should be something there to stop the blinds from falling out of the end? A trip to the spare room, where the blinds had been stored, revealed the answer – there on the floor was a piece of plastic shaped to fit inside the bar, and a tiny plastic ring with a wee screw to hold it in place. Problem solved? Alas, no. Because these blinds have been sitting in the sun (which is, after all, their job) the plastic has become brittle and the wee retaining ring shattered into four pieces when I tried to fit it.

Result – a temporary bodge with insulating tape and an on-line visit to my friend Mr Amazon to order a whole new blind. Thank goodness my pension came through at the end of the month.

Because of the vertical blind shenanigans, I missed popmaster. Yes, really! But not to worry, a few weeks ago I had the foresight to set my Sky box to record Radio 2 between 10.25 and 11.00 every morning for just such occasions as these. So I settled down in front of the telly with my mug of tea, selected "planner" and pressed play. And I got off to a flying start. The Round 1 contestant picked "sounds of the 70s" as his bonus subject, right up my street, and I was soon romping ahead on the scoreboard.

However, after I'd smashed the Donna Summer question, sailed through the Alvin Stardust one and was approaching the Elvis Presley one, I began to feel that this was all a little too easy and slightly familiar, almost as if I'd heard these questions before. Peering forward and squinting at the screen I realised I was answering the questions I'd recorded (and answered) on the 24th of March. I really do need to get my eyes tested.

But it wasn't a total disappointment, as you'll see by the score at the bottom of the page. When I finally got tuned into the recording of today's popmaster the second contestant picked "The Rolling Stones" for his bonus questions. This was a gift for me and I answered all his bonus questions easily, plus three others.

Six mile walk again this afternoon, that's two days in a row. Ooh my poor ankle, thank goodness for the newly purchased paracetomol.

Popmaster score: Round 1 – 9 points Round 2 – 27 points.

23

Social Distancing Diary – Day 20, a day of surprises. Behind the fridge.

Saturday comes around again, and with it a real sense of "groundhog day". Same routine as yesterday, and the day before, and tomorrow too. So no trip to town, no supermarket breakfast, no takeaway coffee. On the plus side, I'm trying to think of the money I'm saving, and the health benefits. But mostly I'm thinking about the breakfast.

When M got up this morning she observed a strange bulky shape through the outside glass door. When she opened it she was confronted by the scabby cat from Day 17. Not lurking under the hedge, but sitting brazenly on the doorstep. I was still in bed, but I heard the thundering footsteps and high decibel threats as the unfortunate puss was "actively encouraged" to leave".

In 2008 we bought a fridge freezer, which fits snugly in its own space in the kitchen, and which hasn't been moved since it was first installed. This weekend, of course, it had to be pulled out from its cosy nook to allow for the wall behind it to be painted. Believe me friends, it's infinitely better not to know what's lurking behind your fridge. We retrieved a vast range of items including, but not limited to, a huge collection of fluff, a leaking AAA battery, a couple of dried-up plums (though they might have started life as satsumas) and a 5p coin dated 2012. Everything went in the bin, except the five pence, which automatically became my property and is now safely in my piggy bank.

Also being subjected to the painting regime are the door surrounds, which inevitably requires the removal of the doors. So - immediately after breakfast - there I was, screwdriver in hand, wrestling with screws which haven't been wrestled with for some twenty years. Unfortunately for me we have two internal doors leading into (or out of) the kitchen. One has been removed for today, and once the paint has dried it will have to be replaced tomorrow. The other one will be done on Monday. Something to look forward to? I can't wait.

Much to their delight, the early potatoes are finally in the ground! It was a nice warm morning so I took the opportunity to release them from captivity and plant them in the newly cultivated veggie plot. They're planted about four inches or so deep, unlike when I was first married and learning about gardening, and planted them about a foot down. Later that year my auntie in Australia phoned to say she was fairly enjoying my tatties.

Afternoon exercise saw us walking into Dingwall, to get the weekly electric meter top-up. I always have to wait outside while M goes into the shop. I've forgotten what it actually feels like to go inside a shop. I stood outside, with my nose pressed to the window, until the shopkeeper came out and told me to clear off because I was steaming up the glass. And scaring the customers.

Luckily, that shop also sells newspapers so M very kindly bought me a Scotsman and a Times. That will keep me in crosswords for at least the next five days.

M has been missing her football on the telly, and has been lamenting the poor quality of some of the shows on offer. Last night however, she was much happier because on BBC2 at 8.30 was Gardener's World, which she recorded to watch tonight as a special Saturday night treat. The show usually features the Blessed Saint Monty of Don but sadly he's in self-isolation so not appearing for a couple of weeks.

Meanwhile I should have been watching last summer's Runrig concert on YouTube, hoping to spot myself in the crowd. Alas it too has been postponed for a week.

No Popmaster today because it's Saturday. But I got four out of five questions right in the Daily Mirror's "daily pub quiz".

24

∾

Social Distancing Diary – Day 21, a day of rest.

Welcome to Sunday, a day of rest in the Thomson household where anything remotely strenuous is banned, including painting. But not, apparently, long distance walking.

The kitchen door from yesterday has been successfully re-hung. Right way up and right way round, remarkably. While the hinges were off I took the opportunity to give them a clean up and a coat of oil, so no more squeaking. This makes it much easier for me to sneak into the kitchen and raid the fridge after M has gone to bed.

Another day, another crossword, Scotland on Sunday this time. And I learnt where Abertawe is, and what my maxilla is. Every day's a school day.

I also learnt that the time lapse between settling down with the Sunday paper and falling asleep is something less than four minutes.

Success on the garden supplies front! Fortuitously a catalogue arrived the other day, from a company we've dealt with in the past but had quite forgotten about. I immediately logged on to their website and hoorah! They were happy to accept my order, and even happier to accept my credit card details. Some items are already winging their way to me, while others will be sent at the appropriate time for planting. So our meagre potato/beetroot diet will be enhanced by a wide variety of vegetables, and M's containers and hanging baskets will be as colourful as ever. The neighbours will be well jel, as we youngsters say.

In other garden news, I had hoped that yesterday's potatoes would be fully grown and ready for harvesting by today. They were described as an early variety, but obviously not that early.

Six mile walk this afternoon, really nice day so lots of joggers, cyclists and dog walkers around. The first three or four miles is tarred road, which fortunately meets the UK standard width of 3.5 metres, so distancing isn't a problem. Not for the people anyway, but the dogs don't much like being restrained, when all they want to do is come up close for a cuddle or a treat. In normal times we're happy to give them both so I hope they remember that when these restrictions are over.

There's a horse riding centre near our village so we always pass a couple of fields with horses. One particular pony came to the fence today to greet us and was obviously offended that we hadn't brought anything with us for him to eat. The offer of a doggy treat was rejected with a scornful snort and a disparaging look down his (impressively long) nose. Note to self – remember to bring a carrot on the next walk.

I mentioned a couple of days ago that I need to get my eyes tested. Not only that, but I was due to have my annual asthma review in March, and a six-monthly dental check-up. All of these routine things are on hold until after lockdown. So if you're out for your walk and you spot a toothless, wheezing, squinting pensioner with a sore ankle, that'll be me.

25

ᏜᏜ

Social Distancing Diary – Day 22, a day of make do and mend

Had a bit of a sleepless night, feeling very warm. Fears that it might be caused by the virus were allayed when we checked the temperature – a massive 13 degrees C. In April. In the north of Scotland. In this area April is often a month of frosts, snow showers, rain showers, and high winds. Just like every other month of the year.

The second kitchen door has now been removed to have its surrounds painted. That's the painting all done now. M has used up all the paint stocks she's been hoarding for months so all that remains is to refit that door tomorrow and we can get back to normal, ie not having to avoid touching walls/door frames, and not hearing the cries of: "watch the paint!" whenever heading to the toilet/kitchen/beer cupboard.

My letter from the Government has finally arrived. "Dear Sandy", it begins: "Thank you for writing your diary, you and The Queen are both doing a great job of keeping our spirits up".

It goes on to give advice about symptoms, isolation and hand washing. My own hands are very sore with all this extra washing. I have to use a moisturiser a couple of times a day to stop them drying out. The moisturiser I have on prescription is paraffin based and highly inflammable, so I have to be careful to avoid naked flames after I've applied it. Luckily I don't smoke, or I might go up in smoke. And no candles allowed on my birthday cake.

Speaking of birthdays, a few weeks ago when it was my actual birthday M very generously gave me a gift of some clothing. Look away now if you're of a nervous disposition because certain items come under the category of "underwear". OK, boxer shorts if you must know. These particular garments were made in France, and I guess French men must be less sensitive than I am because they had a very jaggy laundry label sewn towards the rear, in a very irritating location.

The offending label had to be removed, and fast, before it caused an irritation in a very sensitive area. I got the sewing scissors out and carefully unpicked the stitches securing the label, only to find that they were in fact part of the stitching on the rear seam, therefore there was a small but gaping hole left, in an embarrassing location.

And I've always been of the opinion that one's underwear must always be in perfect condition, hole-free at least, in case of being run over by a bus and taken to hospital. Not that there's much chance of being run over by a bus around here. You'd have to wait a long time before throwing yourself under the number 27 for Inverness.

Fortunately I'm blessed with sewing skills, which I learnt at my granny's knee, and I was able to neatly and accurately sew up the seam. The sewing took about three minutes and threading the needle took at least ten. At the window, with my tongue sticking out and one eye shut. Heaven knows what the neighbours must have thought.

Nice surprise this afternoon – after a long absence El Gato has returned! Have to admit we've been worrying about him so, in a gesture of friendship in these troubled times, M has put out a saucer of milk and bread for him. We're hoping that if we provide him with snacks he'll leave the birds alone.

Ankle very sore today, so M did the long walk and I did a short one. And because I'm much slower than she is, we arrived home within minutes of each other. Beautiful weather, so lots of people and dogs out but everyone being very sensible here.

Popmaster score: Round 1 – 3 points Round 2 – 3 points

26

～

Social Distancing Diary – Day 23, a day of rocks and rainbows

During the current crisis the rainbow seems to have become the symbol of hope. I've been seeing them in house windows, obviously drawn by kids, and in our local care home windows, drawn by our senior citizens. I'm nearer to one of those age groups than I am to the other, so I thought perhaps I could make a contribution to this brightening up of our environment. I had three flat stones lying around which had once been painted on and bought at craft fairs, but the original artworks had long since worn off. And all three were of a suitable shape, I thought, for me to paint a rainbow on. And anyway, I passed O'Grade Art in 1967 so I'm well qualified.

So, digging in the bowels of the Shed From Hell, I unearthed some tubes of acrylic paint which I'd been storing for years, "in case they might come in handy one day". Just goes to show you should never throw anything away. Drew some arch shapes on the stones and began planning how to paint them. Then came the question – what are the colours of the rainbow? Everybody knows that except, apparently, me. Easy, I thought : "yellow, green, brown, blue, pink, black". Until I realised that's the order for potting snooker balls, not painting rainbows.

Then I remembered the well-known song and began to sing it in my head: "Red and yellow and erm, something and something, erm, something and something and blue". No, that wasn't going to help either. Finally, somewhere in the deepest recesses of my brain I dragged up a memory from when M Junior was in school and learning this very thing. The acronym she used was ROY G BIV and so my dilemma was solved. With my limited range of primary colours ROY G and B were easy, I and V less so. My first attempts at mixing resulted in delicate shades of muddy brown and grotty grey, until I worked out that both colours were a mixture of red and blue but in different proportions. I suppose I must have known that in 1967.

I'm happy to say I got there in the end, nice bright colours and a coat of clear varnish, and now our doorstep is enhanced by a rainbow stone on either side, and there's one on the front window sill to cheer passers by. I can hear their comments now: "Ooh look, the Thomsons must have adopted a five-year old child".

Still on a stony theme, we have a central bed in the middle of what passes for a lawn, surrounded by a low dry stone wall. Built by me several years ago, from old cobblestones. Due to the wet winter the whole area was flooded for weeks on end, and part of the wall collapsed. Repairing this has been on my "to do" list for a number of weeks (well, sixteen is a number) and I've been relying on that old faithful excuse favoured by men everywhere: "...waiting for better weather".

Today was dry and sunny, with a healthy breeze. "A great drying day", as my granny would have said. So no more excuses, the wall had to be tackled. Phew it was heavy work. In the intervening years either the cobbles have become heavier, or I've become older and weaker. I think we all know which is correct.

Anyway, after much bending and grunting - and some choice expressions in both English and Gaelic - the wall is finally repaired and hopefully will remain standing until the next floods. Which will probably arrive next week.

Finished Saturday's Times crossword today, three days after starting it. And it's not even the jumbo one, it's just the standard Times cryptic one. I shall start the jumbo one tonight and try to finish it before next Saturday.

Popmaster score: Round 1 – 6 points Round 2 – 12 points

27

⌘

Social Distancing Diary – Day 24, a day of downpours. And a wee mouse.

Beautiful spring morning, so up early, washing machine on and washing hung out. The neighbours are impressed.

An hour later – heavens open, pouring rain, washing hastily retrieved whilst getting soaked. The neighbours are amused.

And that just about set the scene for the day. Heavy rain all morning, although I did manage a dry walk. Showers in the afternoon so I stayed in while M went out on her own for her long walk. When she came home she left her wet jacket to dry in the greenhouse. I wondered why she hadn't hung it in her shed and she revealed that she'd encountered a wee mouse in there this morning while she was tidying up. I don't know which of them got the biggest fright but she wouldn't leave her jacket in the shed in case the mouse would make a nest in the pocket and proceed to have multiple babies.

I expect that now spring is here the mousie will be moving outdoors in search of food, and a place to raise a mouse family.

There's no food in the shed, although there is a fridge with some emergency beer in it. He'd better not be touching that.

Selflessly kept aside some cooked chicken from last night's dinner, for El Gato to have with a saucer of milk. This morning when I carried out my daily inspection of the Prize Vegetable Patch I was horrified to find evidence of some creature having been digging, surrounded by paw prints, suspiciously cat-shaped. I suspect El Gato has buried a little "surprise" for me to find when I'm digging up the tatties. There's gratitude for you. Or is it catitude?

I really need to watch my diet during lockdown, otherwise I'll need to invest in a larger size of jeans with stretch waistbands. I've been trying very hard to eat healthily but it's very easy to reach for the biscuit tin. Especially on a day like today, when rain forces me to stay indoors. This morning I was doing so well, with cereal, fruit and yoghurt, until the phone rang. It was my elderly Italian neighbour inviting me round to collect a cake and a batch of scones she'd made for me.

In spite of my protests about ruining my figure she insists that I don't eat enough. Apparently the average Italian eats much more than I do but she tends to forget that there's a difference between the two diets. The Italian diet consists largely of fruits, fish, beans, tomatoes and whole grains, while mine consists mainly of chips, beer, chocolate, cakes and scones. And Harry Gow's dream rings.

Speaking of which, Harry Gow's shop has temporarily closed. And to add insult to injury, the other baker in Dingwall William Deas, has also shut down for the duration. My top t favourite things in this world are dream rings from Harry Gow and mince pies from Deas, so you can understand my devastation.

It must have been similar when rationing was imposed during the war, although that was much worse, with essentials like meat, sugar and butter being rationed. At least we can always get the basics,now that panic buying seems to have subsided.

We even have toilet roll, which means I no longer need to go out after dark and steal cabbage leaves from neighbours' gardens.

Popmaster score: Round 1 – 21 points Round 2 – 6 points

28

~~

Social Distancing Diary – Day 25, a day of mechanical success

Paper and plastic recycling bin gets collected every two weeks, and today I was glad to see it getting emptied because it contained all the out of date publications and assorted papers I told you about on Day 11. I hope the man at the recycling depot has a 20-year-old Indesit washing machine. He'll enjoy reading the instruction manual.

I must admit I feel rather jealous of the recycling bin. It gets taken out more often than I do.

Exciting news! Harry Gow, the baker of dream ring fame, has announced that due to overwhelming demand he's starting a delivery service. And, in addition to the usual bread, rolls etc he's including dream rings. In fact he mentioned them specifically. Sadly deliveries are limited to the Inverness area at present but I'm hopeful that he'll expand into my wee corner of Ross-shire before too long.

I didn't realise I was so famous for my obsession with dream rings until the news broke this morning and I received personal messages from a number of my friends telling me about it. Oh dear, you all know me too well. And if any of you actually know Harry Gow, please tell him about my diary and frequent mentions of him. Maybe, just maybe, he'll bung me a couple of dream rings for free.

Today was a mechanical day. The grass is beginning to grow and will need cutting soon, so it was time to give the lawnmower its annual service. Actually this should have been done long ago. Every year in November, newspaper garden articles always advise: "now's the time to service and clean up your mower before putting it away for the winter". Well, I must have been too busy that week because it didn't get done until today.

Spark plug removal involves much fiddling, muttering and skinned knuckles. Air filter removal involves much fiddling, muttering and inhaling last year's dried grass. Removing the blade for sharpening involves much fiddling, muttering and (very nearly!) finger amputation. Anyway I got there in the end, fresh fuel installed and ready to start the engine. This is always a tense time, which often results in the neighbours learning some new and interesting phrases.

I noticed M watching from a safe distance, ie the bedroom window, with the swear box in hand. Pulling the starting cable, I began to count. Usually it takes dozens of pulls, with lots of rest breaks, to get the engine to fire but today – rejoice – it started at the sixteenth pull! So no contributions to the swear box, but I did notice M kept it handy because she knew the strimmer was next for servicing.

As it turned out, the strimmer caused no problems at all. A wee plug and filter clean-up, some fresh fuel and it started after eight pulls. So, feeling very smug, I put them both back in their shed. I don't suppose I'll be feeling so smug when the grass grows and I have to start using them every week.

Been resting the ankle for a couple of days, only having short walks, so today I tried the six-miler with M. Managed it OK and it was a nice dry day. Quite busy though, especially on the tarred road section. We encountered various cyclists, a couple of joggers, a motorcyclist and a large white horse. The latter two each had a rider on board, thankfully.

And everyone crosses the road to give each other two metres of space. This is no novelty for me, because for as long as I can remember people have always crossed the road to avoid me.

And to finish the day off with a laugh – Susan Calman on the BBC Scotland channel with guests Farmer J, Dog F and a new one – Chicken B!

Popmaster score: Round 1 – 9 points Round 2 – 18 points

29

_∾_

Social Distancing Diary – Day 26, a day of painting. By me for a change.

Today is Good Friday so I thought I ought to do something good. M has been doing good things ever since lockdown started. Having finished all her painting and decorating she turned her attentions to cleaning out the kitchen cupboards. You might imagine some of the stuff she found, including a half-full bag of brown sugar and the dregs of some vanilla extract, last seen a few years ago when I decided it was time to learn a new skill, and baked a batch of biscuits. The recipe was from an American website, so it was actually a batch of cookies.

And whether you call them biscuits or cookies, there was no disguising the fact that they were a little on the "hard" side. In fact they were so "hard" that I could have used them to repair the wall which fell down last winter. Perhaps I should have stuck to the recommended fifteen minutes instead of adding a further ten "just to be sure". Good business for the dentist though. Everyone who tried one broke at least one tooth.

M also found two packs of teabags labelled "souvenir of London". "Yes", she said, "I remember buying these when the Olympics were in London, a couple of years ago". A quick check with Professor Google confirmed that the Olympics were in London not "a couple of years ago" but in 2012, nearly eight years ago. However I've been drinking the tea since yesterday with no ill effects. Apart from holding a medal ceremony - complete with national anthem - every time I have a cup.

Anyway, for my Good Friday activity, immediately after Popmaster I got busy with the paint brush. Yes, really, my most hated of all activities, apart from rainbows of course. Some years ago I put up a small fence along one end of what used to M's flower garden but which is now my Prize Vegetable Patch. Just a simple wee fence with spars and boards and only about three feet high. Originally painted green, it had faded to a dull and ugly grey. After a generous application of wood preserver it's now back to its original lustrous green, dull and ugly no more. Unlike myself. I fear it would take more than a coat of paint to restore me to my original state.

Incidentally the paint has the brand name "Ronseal". The Gaelic speakers amongst you will know that "ròn" in Scottish Gaelic means "seal" (the aquatic mammal, not the pop singer). Therefore I appear to have painted my fence with a product called "Sealseal". Or, in Gaelic, "Ronròn".

And now that I was in the mood there was no stopping me! I found an old tin of clear Cuprinol (no seals here) and began coating my garden shed with it. Sadly I only had enough to do one end of the shed, but when lockdown is over and we're allowed to go shopping again I shall buy another tin.

And I'll do the other three walls. In a year or two. When the weather's better.

Having devoted a chunk of my life to serving HMG (Her Majesty's Government), not HMV (His Master's Voice, although that might have been more fun), I'm happily in receipt of a modest pension. Yesterday a communication arrived from the pension administrators telling me I'm due to receive an "annual PI". At first I thought it must be a misprint, and I got excited about receiving an annual PIE, but sadly PI turns out to stand for "Pensions Increase".

Oh well, I consoled myself, no pie but surely a considerable enhancement coming my way. However the small print reveals my PI to be a less than eye-watering £3.56 per month. And that's before the tax man takes his share. I suppose I should be grateful, but it won't buy many pies.

In other news, I see the UK Government message for Easter weekend is "stay home". Even I, who failed Higher English in spectacular fashion in 1968, know that in British English it should read "stay AT home". Either way, please do it. And wash your hands. And happy Easter.

Popmaster score: Round 1 – 3 points Round 2 – 9 points

30

～

Social Distancing Diary – Day 27, a day of shed culture

Another Saturday, another morning walk, another load of washing, another day without a cooked breakfast. It's getting very hard to know what day it is. If it wasn't for M buying me The Times I wouldn't have a clue.

A look at last Saturday's diary reminds me that it's now a full week since I planted the early potatoes. Every day I go out and stare hopefully at the ground, willing them to make an appearance but still no sign of them. A Google search tells me that one cause of potato crop failure is too much nitrogen. I wonder whether El Gato's "truffles" have a high nitrogen content.

Today was a shed-clearing day. We have "His" and "Hers" sheds, plus a wee plastic one for the lawnmower. "Hers" is always in a mess, very untidy and full of stuff which hasn't been needed for years and probably never will be. Until the day after we throw it out. It's not entirely M's fault because that's the shed into which I throw anything which might make mine untidy. No wonder she's got mice.

So, immediately after breakfast, M launched herself into a major shed-clearing frenzy. Stuff was getting thrown out with such velocity it got to the stage where I was afraid to walk past the door. Garden tools were evicted, and instructed to be stored in the mower shed. A bag of winter grit was ejected, and had to be stored in a plastic dustbin previously used for rabbit food. And even an old desk lamp was ditched. Luckily I managed to salvage the hundred-watt bulb out of it before it was chucked in a box for when the recycling centre opens again.

My shed,on the other hand, is my domain and my refuge from the world. No-one is allowed to enter without permission, except when they're bringing me tea or food. Or both. It's also very tidy, with all my woodworking and other tools carefully stored, and everything is in its place. It's also carpeted and has a radio and a stool, and that's where I achieve some of my best Popmaster scores.

My woodworking tools include a couple of handsaws made by Spear and Jackson. Their model name is "Predator" and when I bought them they had a special offer running – buy two saws and get a free baseball cap. Well I can't resist a freebie so that's why I bought two saws. And the baseball cap turned out to be plain black with the model name on the front. At that time I was working in a secondary school in Inverness, and I thought it was probably best not to wear the hat to work. In a building containing a thousand teenagers, a man wearing a black baseball cap emblazoned with the word "Predator" in big red letters might just have conveyed the wrong message. And would probably have earned me a mention, with photo, on the front page of the Highland News.

M's shed, however, is the only one with electricity, which is why the emergency beer fridge lives in there. It wasn't bought as a beer fridge of course, its original purpose was for storing kale and salad leaves for the various rabbits and guinea pigs we've had over the years. Now that we have no small animals it's very handy as an overspill fridge for food from the house fridge and for cooling the jellies when I make my legendary Birds Trifles. But mostly it's for my emergency beer. Which is so called because if I'm working outside and I have an emergency, I can get access to beer without having to take my boots off to come into the house.

And emergencies come in many forms. Cut my finger on the Predator saw – Emergency! Tatties haven't come through the ground – Emergency! Scored less than ten at Popmaster – Emergency!

No Popmaster today of course, but there was a Runrig concert live on Facebook tonight. Recorded in Stirling in August 2018, it was a great experience being there on the day, and I was hoping that the camera would spot me at some point. But not when I was in an embarrassing position, eg guzzling beer or scoffing burgers. Or, worse, queueing for the toilet with my legs crossed.

31

⁓

Social Distancing Diary – Day 28, a day of eggy memories. And surprises.

And it's Sunday again! Not just any Sunday, but Easter Sunday.

Today's the day for kids to roll their eggs. A traditional activity, which still hasn't quite died down in this part of the country and which I remember from my own childhood. Easter wasn't complete until you had: a) dropped at least one egg before it even reached the pan, b) scalded the skin off your hands trying to paint your egg before letting it cool, and c) clarted your clothes/face/dog with over enthusiastic applications of paint.

I grew up in a remote part of the Scottish Highlands surrounded by some pretty serious mountains, so there was never any problem finding a hill to roll your egg down. The problem was that it was a traditional sheep farming area, so by the time your egg had come to rest it had passed through a wide range of sheepy bodily fluids and solids. And we still had to eat the offending egg, even if the shell had broken and it was now covered in distinctive (and pungent) brown/yellow stains. Remember the war was still fresh in adults' memories at that time, and "waste not, want not" was the policy in most families.

Anyway, it never did me any harm or had any lasting effects. Apart from a compulsion to run away whenever I see a collie dog. And an allergy to mint sauce.

Spent a very happy three hours last night watching the recording of Runrig's "Last Dance" concert from 2018. With the earphones on, of course, so as not to disturb M's viewing of Gardener's World, which she watches earnestly in the hope that The Blessed Monty has emerged from his self isolation. Sadly he's still absent from duty. I will be first to know when he's back because the cheers from the sofa will be deafening, even with my earphones on.

But to get back to the Runrig concert, it was lovely to relive the experience, and I spotted a few friends amongst the audience. It was nearly as good as actually being there although there was no hot dog stand or beer bar. And the toilet queue was slightly shorter.

Sunday today, so no shed clearing / painting or any other strenuous activity. But when I opened my shed today to fetch my stick for my morning walk there was, as they say in Asda, an "unexpected item" on the workbench. Closer examination identified it as a large chocolate Easter egg, alongside a newspaper cutting of a cute bunny photo. Obviously the Easter Bunny is a "key worker", and was out last night delivering his eggs around the village.

Either that or M sneaked out to my shed last night whilst I

was engrossed in full-volume Runrig reminiscences. She denies it, of course, but I really can't imagine a real rabbit walking around with a basket of chocolate eggs, can you? And where does he get the eggs from, does he lay them himself? The more I think about it the less attractive this chocolate egg becomes.

I'm still resting this ankle so had my usual short walk today, while M went solo on the six-mile circuit. That's three days in a row I've swerved the long one, and I fear it's beginning to have an effect on my waistline. So I expect M will insist on me taking part tomorrow. She says that if I want to stay at home again that's fine by her. But she'll be taking the biscuit tin with her.

32

〜

**Social Distancing Diary – Day 29, a day of DIY distur-
bance**

Bit of a sleepless night last night, not helped by being rudely
disturbed after going to bed, by a very loud and alarming sound
from the kitchen. I was just nicely settled with my book, (The
Long Drop by Denise Mina, if you must know) when – crash!
The heart-stopping sound of something falling from a great
height! First thought was – "how did El Gato get into the house?
The windows are closed and we don't have a cat flap!"

There was no cat, of course. A strip of wood with hooks on,
which is used for hanging chopping boards and other utensils,
had come away from the wall and was lying forlornly on the
floor, surrounded by its former attachments. I wouldn't have
minded, but I took it down and rehung it only last week, during the kitchen painting session. What I should have realised, of
course, is that in the period between the original fitting and now,
the plastic rawlplugs it was screwed into had become brittle and
were no longer able to grip the screws.

Amidst much ribbing from M, and wry comments about "O Grade Woodwork, eh?" I sheepishly inserted new rawlplugs and reinstalled the hanger. My only excuse is that I sat my O Grades in 1967 and the plastic rawlplug didn't reach my remote part of the Highlands until 1968. This may not strictly be true, but it's the best I could come up with.

Easter Bank Holiday Monday! Must say, it doesn't feel at all like a bank holiday. It was very cold on my morning walk, and of course there's hardly any traffic so the roads are spookily quiet. I had a couple of close encounters with nature this morning in the woods. Firstly a young roe buck, standing so still that I almost didn't notice him. He was only a couple of metres away, with a casual disregard for government warnings about social distancing.

Anyway, once he realised he'd been spotted he moved away, but not in any great hurry. Obviously he had performed a risk assessment upon me and discounted me as being any kind of threat. On the roe deer threat level chart I imagine "pack of lions" is at the top, followed by "gamekeeper with gun", and so on. I expect "pensioner with walking pole" comes towards the bottom of the list.

Then, a little later, in a different part of the woods, two female roe deer. They were much more active, bounding away as soon as they saw me. I think they'd been hanging around casually, hoping to bump into the young male, just like teenage girls used to do when I was that age. And, just like those very same teenage girls all those years ago, they were very disappointed when it turned out to be me.

Having cleared out her shed the other day, M has now decided to give it a coat of fresh paint. It has always been a reddish-brown colour but the only outdoor paint she has in stock is a kind of pale blue-green. When applied, and with the old paint shining through, it gives the shed a very fashionable "distressed" look.

I took a cup of tea out to her after popmaster, and she suggested I might like to help move some heavy paving slabs which were lying around and getting in her way. After I'd completed this task with much muttering and grunting, it wasn't only the shed which looked "distressed".

The sun came out in the afternoon and it became much warmer, so I joined M in her long walk. Afterwards she went back to apply another coat of paint to the shed. Obviously I was far too fatigued to help, but I did run out a couple of times with regular supplies of tea for her. Maybe I should have studied hospitality rather than woodwork. It's much less dangerous.

Popmaster score: Round 1 – 3 points Round 2 – 3 points

33

~~~

Social Distancing Diary – Day 30, a day of technological success. Eventually.

Here we are in the fourth week of lockdown. Both the UK and the Scottish governments are, for once, in agreement that lockdown is working so it looks like it's going to be continued for a few more weeks. I fear that by the time it's over I shall have forgotten how to interact with people. Apart from M, and an occasional 2-metre chat with my neighbour, all my communications have been by text, email or Facebook. Definitely going to need a digital detox once this is over.

And it has become instinctive now to steer clear of anyone you meet outside, even if you know them. I'm worried that this instinct will continue and I'll gain a reputation for being an antisocial, unapproachable old curmudgeon. Oh wait, that's the reputation I had before lockdown, so I don't suppose anyone will know the difference.

What I do worry about is that I may have forgotten how to drive. I went into the car the other day, just to start it up and give the engine a warm up. I only realised how long it's been since I drove when I noticed that the clock hadn't been put forward for British Summer Time. How will I cope? Where does the petrol go? Which is the brake pedal? What side of the road do we drive on?

Schools went back today, after their Easter break. Not physically back of course, but carrying out online learning using technology. Pupils have to register online before 12.00 every school day. I don't know what happens to them if they play truant, or chew gum in class? Do they get sent out of the room? Or kept behind after school? And do teachers run classes in their jammies? I think we should be told.

Saw M Junior today, for the first time in several weeks! Worry not, it was on a screen using what seems to be the latest fashion accessory, Zoom. Took me ages to get it set up properly, but finally I managed it, and there I was on screen waiting for M Junior to join me. I sent her a text message saying: "I'm logged on waiting for you". Meanwhile M Junior was also on screen, and texting saying: "I'm logged on waiting for you". We appeared to be "zooming" in different directions.

Fortunately M Junior is more adept at ICT than I am, and she soon talked me through the procedures so at last we could see and hear each other. M and I on one half of the screen, and M Junior, Dog F and a couple of chickens on the other. Dog F is supposed to be helping with the sheep but she was on her lunch break. And the chickens are on a permanent lunch break. Which obviously did them good, because by this evening they'd produced their first two eggs. Missed Easter by two days, but well done girls.

Two of our elderly neighbours have the gardeners in this week. One next door and one across the street. It's ok for gardeners to work during lockdown because they don't have close contact with their customers. The customers have to stay inside and communicate through a closed window. I wonder if I can persuade M to give that a try? She will be outdoors, obviously, and I shall be inside, with the biscuit tin.

Both of these chaps are cutting grass, for the first time this year. I'm delaying starting my own grass cutting for as long as possible to give it a chance to recover from a very wet winter. Well that's my excuse anyway because once you start it becomes a weekly chore. Like washing your coffee cup. Or changing your underwear.

After seventy-two hours I finally finished Saturday's Times crossword. I will admit I had to enlist the help of Mr Google for a couple of the answers. I'd never heard of ember days, I thought they might be something to do with firelighting but it turns out they're periods of fasting and abstinence. No wonder I'd never heard of them.

Popmaster score: Round 1 – 6 points Round 2 – 9 points

34

Social Distancing Diary – Day 31, a day of panda-mo-nium

Lovely morning, so M did a washing first thing. After it was hung on the line a very strong wind came along and wrapped most of it around the washing line. Spent most of the morning popping out every ten minutes to straighten it out. I remarked to M that my pants were being blown in the wind. Her response, which I thought was rather unkind, was: "Your pants are well accustomed to strong winds!" Can't think what she means by that.

Hoorah! The garden supplies I ordered a week ago have started arriving! First to be delivered was a batch of Maris Piper seed potatoes, which I shall grow as a main crop. To allow them to sprout, they're lying in a darkened room. Wish I could join them.

But once the time comes they'll be planted out adjacent to their early brothers, who I hope will have made an appearance by then. And they don't need to worry about any late frosts, I have a king size duvet standing by to cover them over with. And it has a bright, bold Lion King duvet cover. That should keep the cats away.

You will remember I had to be helped by M Junior to set up "Zoom" on my computer yesterday. Just to reassure you that I'm not a complete technophobe, I can reveal that I actually have a formal qualification in ICT. It's called the "European Computer Driving Licence", or ECDL, and I dug it out yesterday for old times' sake. I suppose I'll have to send it back at the end of December, once we're out of the EU. I don't imagine Frau Merkel will allow me to tinker with her motherboard.

I was surprised to discover that I actually got the licence in 2004, a massive sixteen years ago, when ICT life was much simpler. There was no Facebook, (2005), Twitter (2006) or YouTube (2007) and Zoom was still just a twinkle in someone's eye. As far as I can remember the ECDL exam was pretty straightforward. We had to know how to switch on, how to switch off, and how to cover the screen quickly if the boss came in while we were playing Lemmings.

But I'm disappointed in my own computer, it keeps asking if I'm willing to accept cookies. I always say "yes please" but so far nothing, not even a wee biscuit.

I note in today's paper that Tian Tian, Edinburgh Zoo's female panda, has failed to get pregnant for the ninth year in a row. The zoo authorities are very disappointed because they've been hoping for a cute baby panda (or two) to boost visitor attendances. Everybody loves a cuddly furry baby, whether it's a lamb, a calf or a penguin in a fur coat.

And according to David Attenborough baby pandas do nothing but eat, sleep and lie around all day. Sounds just like my own lifestyle.

So, because I'm at a loose end right now and available for work, I've written to the zoo management offering my services as a stand-in baby panda. I'm the right size (short-ish) and the right shape (round-ish). I'm very happy to dress up in a panda costume and lie around in the straw for a few hours every day. The visitors will be enchanted with my overdose of cuteness. I'm even prepared to try chewing on some bamboo shoots, as long as I'm allowed to dip them in tomato ketchup.

But if Mummy Panda decides it's time for potty training I'm out of there.

Popmaster score: Round 1 – 15 points Round 2 – 9 points

35

〜

Social Distancing Diary – Day 32, a day of groupworking

It's official. Another three weeks of lockdown. I expect I'll be completely bonkers by the end of this.

Today's horoscope suggested that I: "...might benefit from getting involved in a group project". No sooner said than done, I committed myself to not one but TWO group projects today.

Firstly, and this will help explain my recent and sudden interest in Zoom, M Junior had an idea the other day that it might be fun to have a wee online quiz for her and some of her friends. Guess who was tasked with producing the questions and acting as the quizmaster? Yes, that would be me. So which persona should I adopt? The famously grumpy Jeremy Paxman, the even-tempered Jeremy Vine, or the often controversial Jeremy Clarkson? And why are all British TV quiz hosts called Jeremy?

Since at least two thirds of my contestants are schoolteachers, I decided to model myself on the personality of a benevolent but firm head teacher. Praise where it's due, and punishment for misbehaviour. Sadly, because of social distancing, I was unable to physically send anyone out of the room, but the threat of disconnecting them from my Zoom meeting was enough to ensure proper behaviour.

I hadn't realised quite how much work is involved in making up a quiz. Yes, there are lots of online resources and ready-made "pub quiz" type questions, but when you're aiming to make a quiz enjoyable, and when you know who your audience is going to be, you find that perhaps only one in ten questions is suitable. Some are impossibly difficult – "What does a parsec measure?". Some are potentially controversial – "What is the largest Island in the world, Greenland or Australia?". (I've seen mature adults almost come to blows over that one). And some are ridiculously easy, eg "What colour is an orange?" or "What time is News at Ten?"

How many of you are googling "parsec" and "largest island" right now? Ha!

And if you're googling "what colour is an orange" I suggest you keep very quiet about it.

The other group activity I signed up for was a musical one. In the UK, to show our gratitude for our wonderful NHS staff at this awful time, we've been standing outside our houses publicly applauding them every Thursday evening, and this week it's been suggested that we should honour them with a musical tribute. Led by Skerryvore, one of Scotland's favourite bands, along with some well-known guest artistes, a cracking wee tune called

Everyday Heroes has been written. You can find it if you search online for "Skerryvore and friends".

Skerryvore invited all musicians, both professional and amateur, to join in playing this tune at 8pm tonight. And since I fall naturally into the "amateur" category I decided to get my guitar tuned up and join in. Some of you will know I've been teaching muself guitar for quite a few years now. And after hundreds of hours of intensive practice I've finally attained the level of "complete beginner".

Actually, I've been playing guitar quite a lot recently. I usually keep my guitars out on stands in what M calls the spare room, but which I, ever hopeful, call the music room. However, when the mass decorating extravaganza was taking place a couple of weeks ago I had to put the guitars away. Under the bed or on top of the wardrobe, anywhere out of range of flying emulsion splashes. But I'm back in action now, twanging away enthusiastically, if not particularly tunefully.

To keep you in suspense, I'll provide you with updates on both of those activities in tomorrow's diary.

Popmaster score: Round 1 – 12 points Round 2 – 15 points

36

~

Social Distancing Diary – Day 33, a day of not cutting grass. Or hair.

El Gato is becoming very tame, almost approachable. Every night after the seagulls have gone to bed (or wherever seagulls go after dark, does anyone know?), M puts a wee dish of food on the back doorstep for him. Sometimes a little mince, or sausage, or fish, whatever we had for our tea is what he gets in his dish. He'll be a very sad cat if we ever turn vegetarian.

And in the morning, when M gets up at 6am, she finds the dish empty so pops a little extra into it. Then, when she stands back and closes the door, she can see him through the frosted glass, coming and eating it. If she opens the door he runs away, but not as quickly as he used to. Hardly surprising that he's slowed down, with the amount of food M has been stuffing down his face.

At lunchtime today I dared to take one slice – just one slice – of ham from the fridge, only to be soundly reprimanded:

"That's the cat's ham, not for you"…"You can have as much fruit and veg as you like, but leave the cat's ham alone!"

It was a really nice sunny day, so I thought about cutting the grass. And if it's sunny tomorrow I'll probably think about it again. Undoubtedly the day will come when "thinking" has to be replaced by "doing". Until then I shall comfort myself in the knowledge that I can't get a haircut during lockdown and it's not doing me any harm, so it won't hurt the grass to wait a little longer.

I could do with a haircut though. I like to keep my hair short and neat, but nowadays it's sticking up in all directions. Not so much Donny Osmond, more Donny Trump. In the middle of hurricane season.

And so to the report from last night's group experiences. We had our Zoom-based quiz at 7pm as planned. M Junior set up the meeting herself, obviously saving me a great deal of stress, and once the rest of us joined we had a nice wee gathering of four. Plus three dogs. Me as quizmaster and three "contenders", as Mastermind participants are called. And it worked very well, apart from my screen going blank for several minutes. But that didn't matter because I could still hear them and they, sadly, could see me.

Final scores were 20, 18, and 18 so it was a close competition. We're doing it again next week, but one of M's friends is running it this time so I won't be in charge. And just to add a little extra interest she's demanded that we all have to dress up as "a pop star from any era". My era of course is the 60s and 70s but I can't imagine who I can successfully impersonate from that time. I don't have David Bowie's slim figure, David Cassidy's boyish good looks or, luckily, Tina Turner's legs.

Speaking of music, the Skerryvore public event took place last night at 8pm. At 7.55 I was all set up, outside the newly painted shed, with my laptop, music stand and guitar. I knew it was going to be a little chilly, so I had my woolly hat and fleece on. But by the time I started playing, immediately after the applause at thirty seconds after eight, my hands were as blue as the shed, although not as glossy. That's my excuse for all the dodgy chords anyway.

Luckily none of the neighbours were out so they were spared the assault on their ears.

Anyway, I gamely played on and completed the tune, It was only about three minutes forty seconds long, so not exactly a great feat of endurance. Hardly worthy of a polar explorer's medal. But I was very happy to get back inside, and once I'd thawed out I played through the tune again, just for my own satisfaction. And actually got some of the chords right this time.

Popmaster score: Round 1 – 15 points Round 2 – 6 points

37

∾

Social Distancing Diary – Day 34, a day of longing for Ireland

Today, I shouldn't be here. I should be sitting comfortably in a traditional Irish pub, pint of Guinness in hand, immersed in the best of music and craic at the Pan Celtic Festival. Everything was booked, well in advance. Flight from Inverness to Dublin, bus from Dublin to Carlow and a friendly B&B with a comfy bed and a full Irish breakfast. Until Covid-19 intervened and the festival was cancelled. And I'd been dreaming about that full Irish breakfast for the last six months.

The International Pan Celtic Festival is a joyous event. I was last there in 2018 so I had worked out that it was safe to return this year as no-one would be able to remember any outrageous behaviour which might, or might not, have occurred back then. Anyway, outrageous behaviour is not only tolerated at the Pan Celtic, it's expected.

The festival is attended by singers and dancers, musicians and choirs, bands and storytellers from all the Celtic nations,

Ireland, Scotland, Wales, Brittany, Cornwall and the Isle of Man. And each nation has its own language, which is handy because if you start getting your words a wee bit muddled after a few pints of the black nectar, people think you're speaking in your own indigenous tongue. Not that I would know about that, you understand.

There are competitions, concerts, ceilidhs and, of course, sessions in pubs all over town. And it's in the pub sessions that the craic is best. Imagine being in a smallish room with a crowd of Welsh singers in one corner, a Cornish folk band in another and a few local characters sprinkled into the mix. Everybody is everybody else's best friend, everybody contributes to the entertainment and everybody suddenly needs to go to the toilet when I get up to sing. Except for those with hearing aids. Click.

Anyway, thanks Covid-19, you've wrecked my entire year. Every single event I had planned (and, in most cases, booked) for 2020 has been cancelled. Concerts, music festivals, motorcycle races, even the Chelsea Flower Show, all gone. Hurry up 2021, I want my life back.

And so, instead of revelling in Irish hospitality and making new friends, I find myself at home, making friends with the lawn mower. Yes, I've got around to it at last and the grass is cut for the first time. Thanks to my expert servicing the other day, strimmer and mower both started easily. However after fifteen minutes or so the mower engine started emitting smoke from the exhaust and it was only at that point I realised I'd left the choke on. Obviously my mind was elsewhere, still thinking about that Irish breakfast.

On the plus side, while I was cutting the grass M popped into Dingwall to get her electric meter top-up and she brought me a nice present. The Spar shop where she gets the top-ups done also sells alcohol, so she brought home a four-pack of John Smith's Yorkshire Bitter. Other beers are, of course, available but a nice glass of chilled bitter after a busy afternoon is a great joy.

Speaking of gardens, there's some great news in the Thomson household. Yes – MONTY IS BACK! As always, M recorded last night's BBC garden programme to watch tonight, and she's overjoyed to see that the marvellous Mr Don has emerged unscathed from his self isolation and is back in charge. If only the fragrant Joanna would make a reappearance on our screens we'd both be happy.

Six-mile walk this afternoon, so I feel justified in relaxing this evening, with my John Smith's, watching previous Pan Celtic festivals on YouTube and wishing I was there. There's a traditional Irish blessing: "Go n-éirí an bóthar leat" which translates as: "May the road rise to meet you".

And sometimes, on the way home from the pub, it does.

38

Social Distancing Diary – Day 35, a day of garden action. Well, "action" might be stretching it a bit.

A frosty start today. Good for a healthy morning walk, not so good for my lobelia seeds which I sowed in two old biscuit tins a week or so ago. M was chucking out a "Tetley Tea" tin and a "McVitie's Rich Tea" one so I thought that rather than send them to landfill I'd upcycle them. Drilled a few holes in the bottom, filled with seed compost then realised I didn't have any seeds. See, that's what happens if you skimp on the all-important planning process.

Not to be defeated, I carried out a raid on M's greenhouse, with permission, I hasten to add. Rummaged around amongst old plant labels, last year's tomato feed and photos of Monty Don (aha!), and found an old pack of lobelia seeds, dated 2017, with half the contents still present. Using skills that Monty himself would be proud of, I scattered the seed on the compost, covered with cling film as per the instructions on the packet, and placed them beside the window in my shed. Been inspecting them every day since, but no sign of life. And, following the example set by Prince Charles, I've been speaking to them lovingly whenever I'm in the shed. The neighbours were convinced I'd kidnapped a hostage, but because there was never a response they didn't know whether it was male or female. Or feline.

M tells me that lobelia are difficult to grow from seed at the best of times, but even worse in an unheated shed so she's kindly allocated a wee space in the greenhouse for them. She's still dubious about my plant rearing skills but I'm sure that my daily conversations will pay off and I'll be rewarded with a glorious display of blue flowers. And the neighbours can see who I'm talking to, so they no longer think I'm a serial kidnapper. Just a normal everyday lunatic.

Today was the annual "coming out" of the garden bench. We have a wooden bench, bought many years ago, which sits against the house, on the south facing wall. It's a very pleasant spot to sit on a sunny day while you're thinking about cutting the grass. Or not.

But of course a wooden bench is no match for a Highland winter, so every October it gets wrapped up in a protective plastic cover and moved to a sheltered area. Then, in Spring, out it comes again, gets rubbed down and repainted, and reinstalled in its prime position. Much to the relief of the birds, who regard it as their own private perch with en-suite toilet.

I went through a spell over a few years of painting it a different colour every year. It was originally brown, had a spell of being blue, and a couple of years ago I refurbished it with green gloss paint. I thought it looked smart, but M didn't agree, she said it looked like a council bench which we'd nicked from the local park.

She thought the only thing missing was a sign, saying "keep off the grass", or "no ball games". And a grumpy old man sweeping up leaves and being rude to people. Oh, wait...

So once the green paint was sanded off it became brown again, and this year it's still brown, coated with the cuprinol left over from my shed. Drying nicely in the sun today, and ready to be sat upon tomorrow. Unless the birds get there first.

Finally today, I see a story in one of the more sensational Sunday papers about a "secret government masterplan" to reopen some shops, perhaps as early as May 11. The speculation is that these shops include hairdressers, so perhaps there's an end in sight to my Donald Trump hairstyle. Just as I was beginning to search Amazon for a home spray tan kit.

39

∽

Social Distancing Diary – Day 36, a day of credit card heaven

The postie brought the dreaded credit card bill today. For the first time in history, it contained some good news. Chelsea Flower Show tickets – refund arrived. Hotel booking for same – refund arrived. And theatre tickets for our Eden Court shows - refund arrived.

Minimum payment required this month = £0.00. Deep joy.

Still no refund from easyJet though, nor any reply from their helpline. And my Pan Celtic colleague, who paid for our Dublin flights, has had notification from Loganair that their refund period has been extended from 28 days to 60 days. I could probably walk to Dublin in that time, even with my sore ankle.

Also in the postie's bag today was a consignment of lettuce seeds which I ordered a week or so ago. I hadn't realised just how many seeds are in a packet – according to the label there are over a thousand. That's a lot of lettuce for a family of two. Especially since we no longer have a rabbit or guinea pig.

That reminded me that Saturday was the first time in many years when I was able to cut the grass without having to navigate around a rabbit run or guinea pig enclosure. We always allowed our small animals access to the grass, partly because it's the best natural diet for rabbits and guinea pigs, and partly because the more they chomped the less I had to cut.

They always needed supplementary feeding of course. Favourites were kale, carrots and lettuce, all of which we grew but hardly ever tasted. If the animals didn't get them the carrot flies, slugs and caterpillars did.

The main thing I'm looking forward to from the garden company is my tomato plants. They won't come until the appropriate time, maybe another month, but already M has begun revamping the greenhouse to make space for them. We have two greenhouses, one with plants and one full of rubbish, which needs a good sort out. The one with plants is home to M's summer bedding seedlings, which she grows from seed every year and which are coming along nicely, like ten-year-old me being taken to the sweet shop. Unlike my lobelia, which are very reluctant to come at all, like eleven-year-old me being dragged to the dentist.

That's the greenhouse where the tomatoes will eventually go. The other one has become a storage space for all sorts of items, rather like a see-through version of the Shed From Hell. All old plant pots and containers, along with patio furniture, get thrown in there. But I'm confident that once M has finished sorting out her own greenhouse, that one will be next on her list for a clear out. One problem is that the recycling centre is closed at present, so I can't get rid of all the junk she throws out. The wee plastic lawnmower shed is bursting at the seams with wood, plastic and metal junk, all carefully segregated and waiting to be taken to Dingwall. I know how it feels, I also feel very segregated and would love to be taken to Dingwall. There's a phrase I never thought I'd write.

This is the week for the SQA exam materials to arrive in school. Or at least it would have been if Covid-19 hadn't forced the cancellation of the exams. Exam material delivery day is usually an exciting day for me, it's my duty to check all the exam papers, answer papers and other materials, and store them safely in secure cabinets to which only I have the keys. Even the Head Teacher can't get access to my cupboards, which makes me feel very superior. But this year, alas! My cupboards are empty and I miss school. And that's another phrase I never thought I'd write.

Popmaster score: Round 1 – 12 points Round 2 – 3 points

40

~

Social Distancing Diary – Day 37, a day of phone fun

A couple of weeks ago we began having trouble with the landline phone. We rely on it for voice calls because our mobile phones don't work very well around here, and are only used for text messaging.

In the middle of a conversation the phone would suddenly cut out, which was a little inconvenient when chatting with M Junior, but quite welcome when listening to the annoying people who phone me several times a month to discuss my recent accident.

Occasionally, I play along and say: "Ooh yes, I have had an accident", and they get quite excited. Then when they ask me to describe my accident I tell them I was taking eggs out of the fridge for my breakfast and I accidentally dropped one. Usually at that point there's a resounding *click* as they slam the phone down, but sometimes I get one with a sense of humour who plays along. And they have the good grace to laugh when I go on to say: "...and the worst thing of all is that it was a double yolker".

Anyway, it was obviously time for a new phone, so I turned to Argos for help. And they were a great help. Selected a new model, paid online, chose a delivery day and sure enough, it was delivered bang on time. In fact, on the day of delivery I got a text message from Argos "Your delivery is 0 minutes away". I don't know why they bother telling you that, unless they want to make sure their driver doesn't catch you in the toilet. Even then, less than a minute sometimes just isn't long enough to make oneself decent and anyway, who takes their mobile phone into the toilet? Oh, do you?

And once installed, set up and tested, it works beautifully. The only downside is that its cable is about a foot shorter than the previous one, so it has had to be relocated and the breadbin moved. And when it rings I always automatically go to where it used to be, not where it is now and find myself shouting "Hello? Hello?" into a Lidl's croissant. I wouldn't mind so much if it was a Harry Gow's dream ring.

Continuing with the bakery theme, our lovely elderly Italian neighbour often makes cakes and scones, and generously shares them with us. She phones us to let us know, we pop outside and there on the dividing wall is a lovely warm treat. Today it was a few fresh fruit scones so M was very posh this afternoon and treated me to a cream tea. Earl Gray tea, homemade scones, strawberry jam and that most wonderful of all inventions, squirty cream. I thought I was in Heaven. Or maybe it was Devon.

I've been thinking about Thursday night's approaching on line quiz with M Junior and friends. Remember I told you the theme was "a pop star from any era"? Sadly, there are no shops open which sell disguises or dressing-up materials so I've had to get busy and creative and have devised a costume. I can't say too much because M Junior and her friends read this diary but suffice to say it has been made in true Blue Peter style, using materials found around the home. I hope M doesn't notice two eye holes cut out of her favourite pillow case. If she does I shall blame the moths.

It has been a very nice day here. After pottering around all morning I decided I'd accompany M on the six mile walk this afternoon. Very pleased to see the farmers are taking advantage of the good weather to finish off sowing their spring barley. And why am I so pleased? Well, most of the barley in this area goes for malting. And malt becomes whisky. And malt whisky makes me smile. Except when I have to pay for it.

Popmaster score: Round 1 – 3 points Round 2 – 9 points

41

～

Social Distancing Diary – Day 38, a day of wedding memories

A disturbed sleep last night. Awoke at 1.00am to a terrible noise outside the bedroom window. Which is unusual, because the terrible noises in this house usually happen inside the bedroom. Especially if I've been on the beer, and sleeping on my back.

Anyway, this noise was bloodcurdling, hissing and meowling, evidently two cats having a really violent fight. I suspect one of them was El Gato, and the other one probably that scabby cat which visits occasionally. We leave a dish of food on the back doorstep for El Gato at dusk every night, he usually arrives just as it's getting dark, but last night he must have been delayed and discovered the scabby one helping himself to the food. And instead of saying: "I say, old chap, do you mind?" in cat language, he obviously launched himself into a full attack with all the fury of a pack of angry lions.

I understand how he feels, I'm very protective of my food.

Anyone who tries to steal a chip off my plate risks losing a finger. And if you go for a bite of my bacon butty you'll end up pinned to the wall with my free hand while I go on eating with the other one.

Today is an important day for two reasons. Firstly, it's important because this is the training day for my invigilation team. Of course it's not happening now, but I was all prepared for it. I had booked the room in school, had replies from all twenty of my team to say they were able to attend and, most importantly, had arranged with our wonderful SQA Co-ordinator to provide tea and cakes.

It's compulsory for invigilators to attend a training day every year, close to the start of the exam diet. For the new ones it's a chance to meet everyone and learn what invigilation is all about. For the experienced ones it's a chance to catch up with the news, who's been where on holiday, who's got a new grandchild and, as we all get older, who's waiting for an operation (last year it was me).

And I had spent a few hours preparing what I hoped was an exciting and informative training session for them. The usual format is that the SQA Co-ordinator, who is also a Depute Head Teacher, gives them a briefing about how the school operates, ie what the bells sound like, where the toilets are, what to do if the fire alarm sounds (save the cakes!). Then I take over and lecture them for a few hours on the finer points of SQA procedures and regulations.

To keep them interested, anyone still awake at the end of that session is declared the winner and is allowed an extra toilet break during Higher Human Biology. Which is a long exam. And sometimes has a question about the urinary tract. And believe me, that's all it takes.

The other reason today is special is that it's my (and M's!) wedding anniversary. Thirty-seven years ago today we were joined together by the FP minister in Dingwall. I promised to "love, honour and deal with any spiders", and M promised to "love, honour, cook, wash, dust, vacuum, put out the bins and buy all the beer." That may not be exactly how it was, but that's certainly how it turned out.

I remember it well, of course. Don't we all, guys? It was a day not unlike today, dry and a little breezy, and after the ceremony we marched behind the piper from the church to the hotel for the reception. Fortunately we'd had the foresight to choose a hotel in Dingwall, if we'd chosen one in Inverness we'd have been marching for a lot longer.

I asked M how she felt about the anniversary. I really should have known better than to ask.

Me: "How does it feel dear, living with me for thirty-seven years?"

Her: "Quite familiar. Just like thirty-seven years of lockdown".

Popmaster score: Round 1 – 3 points Round 2 – 12 points

42

Social Distancing Diary – Day 39, a day of zooming

Today is St George's Day. Following yesterday's wedding anniversary I shall refrain from making any jokes about dragons.

Just before bedtime last night I made the mistake of looking at the TV news. I was shocked to see a medical expert proposing that, even after lockdown ends, social distancing might have to continue for the rest of this year. Which means I may be forced to spend summer 2020 lounging around at home, eating too much, drinking too much and generally being idle. Which is exactly how I spent summer 2019. The difference is that last year I was a useless lazy good-for-nothing, and this year I'm a responsible, caring citizen. I might even get a medal.

Our grasp of modern technology knows no limits. Yesterday M had an online "Zoom" meeting with the head teacher and staff from one of her schools, and tonight I had a "Zoom" quiz with M Junior and friends.

The school meeting seemed to go quite well. I kept out of the way while they discussed the effects of lockdown on their school. This is the time of year when they've just had their budgets allocated, and order all their classroom materials for the next school year. But this year, that can't happen. because it's looking likely that schools will remain closed until after the summer break. Amazon reports increased sales of mountaineering equipment as parents climb the walls.

So the meeting didn't contain much in the way of good news, but it gave them a rare chance to see into each other's homes. I overheard lots of discussions about each other's wallpaper, so the meeting wasn't a total waste of time. Although I fear that M may have taken some inspiration from some of her colleagues' colour schemes. Thank goodness B & Q is closed so she can't rush out and stock up with wallpaper and paint.

And so to the quiz. Some general knowledge questions, most of which I got wrong. Then some film questions, most of which I got wrong. Then – the music round, based on the official Popmaster quiz book! Here was my chance to redeem myself, especially since today's real popmaster was very hard indeed. But guess what? Yes, I got most of them wrong too, and finished up a miserable third out of three. Next week's dressing up theme is "a historical figure", or in my case "a hysterical quitter".

I wore my pop star disguise for tonight's quiz. M's inspired idea was that I should choose Elton John, so I created a pair of "zoom" specs as per his Rocket Man song. Simply fashioned out of an old cereal box, painted yellow, red and blue and eye holes aligned to fit my own specs. I paired it with a black "Blues Brothers" type plastic hat, a black teeshirt and a white jacket. I was quite impressed with my disguise and think I should start wearing it on my daily walk.

Rumour would soon get round that Elton has bought a holiday home in our village and is self-isolating here. It would certainly get people talking, and I think I'd get off with it. Until someone asks me to sing. Then you'll see who put the "crock" into crocodile rock.

This afternoon M set off on the long walk, anti-clockwise. I agreed I'd set off clockwise shortly afterwards and meet her in the middle, then we'd walk home together. Sadly I was slightly late due to an "accident". Which was that I "accidentally" dozed off while reading the Daily Mail. By the time I met M she was nine-tenths of the way round, so I only had a short walk. Oh dear, what a shame, I thought, as I treated my sore ankle to some beer-based therapy.

Popmaster score: Round 1 – 3 points Round 2 – 3 points

43

～

Social Distancing Diary – Day 40, a day of horticulture

I can't believe this is Day 40. When I started this daily diary I thought I might manage to keep it going for ten days, or even, at a push, twenty. Yet here we are at forty and counting. An epic length of time, in fact it's of biblical proportions. Forty days and forty nights is the time Jesus spent fasting in the desert. Perhaps if I had fasted in the desert all that time instead of stuffing my face in the kitchen, I wouldn't be needing new jeans with an elasticated waist.

Which, I'm ashamed to admit, M actually bought me. They arrived a few days ago and are very comfy. It's nice being able to breathe with my waistband tied, for a change. And my facial colour has gone from "fire engine red" to a much more acceptable "salmon pink".

She bought them from a mail order company called Atlas For Men. First time I saw their catalogue I misread it as "Alas for men". Or, as four-times-married film star Pamela Anderson might have said: "At last! Four men!"

I forgot to tell you yesterday, but I've given the grass its second cut already. I've decided to try to do it twice a week instead of once. This means that I don't need to collect the clippings, which is handy because our local council has suspended garden waste collections. And it saves me from breathing in clouds of mossy spores when I empty the grass box. My asthma nurse would be pleased about that, if I were able to see her.

And after cutting, I spiked the areas where the winter floods were, to allow some air in, and to help with drainage. I use a four-pronged lawn aerator with hollow tines, which removes plugs of soil. And you need to do it in straight lines so as not to miss any bits. It's really heavy work, especially on a warm day, and as fatigue began to set in the lines became progressively less straight. So the top of the lawn looks well-ordered and evenly patterned, and the bottom looks as if it's been rolled on by a crowd of drunken hedgehogs on a stag do. (That's a "bachelor party", for my American readers).

Another delivery from my garden supplier – a hundred litres of compost and a couple of tomato plants. In the catalogue the compost is sold in 50-litre consignments, so I'd expected it to come in two 50-litre bags. I was surprised when it came in two cardboard boxes, and inside each box is ten 5-litre bags. Maybe they saw my Facebook photo and thought: "poor old chap, he'll never manage to lift a big bag so we'll send him a whole load of little ones".

The tomato plants are in very good condition, considering they were despatched on Monday and arrived on Friday. They were well packed and protected, in boxes marked "live plants, this way up". I just wonder whether they spent their whole journey the right way up. They must pass through a number of depots and several vans so I can't imagine the handlers have time to make sure everything is facing the right way. And in any case they must get thrown around all over the place in the back of the van, especially when they get closer. Considering the state of the potholes around here, I'm surprised the driver arrives the right way up.

Anyway, it's a little early this far north for them to go into a cold greenhouse so they're having a couple of days on the spare bedroom windowsill, then they'll go into M's greenhouse, which has an electric heater and can be kept frost-free. And as they grow and mature throughout the season we'll be here to look after them because this summer, as we all know, no-one's going anywhere.

On a happier note, it's Friday and the weekend starts here! Someone please remind me what a weekend feels like......

Popmaster score: Round 1 – 9 points Round 2 – 6 points

44

～

Social Distancing Diary – Day 41, a day of tapping into the spirit

El Gato now comes every morning and evening and is constantly hungry. He eats every scrap of food we put out for him, and looks for more. He doesn't look thin, so M thinks he may need de-worming. Apparently eating all the time without being thin is a symptom of worms. I must say I don't like the way she's started to eye up my own (well nourished) figure.

I visited Amazon to research worm tablets for cats. There's always a wide choice of things on Amazon and so, to help me make a decision, I always read comments by previous customers. And there's a "question and answer" section too, which can be quite interesting. One of the cat worming products boasts that it deals with all worms, leading to one potential purchaser asking the question: "If I plant this in my garden, will it kill all the worms?"

Postie brought a letter from the Scottish Government. Signed by Nicola Sturgeon, it contains encouraging comments and helpful advice. She mentions Scots having "determination, character and compassion" and asks us to be "tapping into that spirit once again". I'm all in favour of tapping into spirit, thanks Nicola.

To help with my determination I'm "determined" to start tapping into Glenfiddich, then if I move on to some Macallan that will surely define me as a "character". And finally, to show some "compassion" I'll shed a wee tear as I drain the last of the Glenmorangie.

Today, as threatened, I cut the grass again without the collecting box. I was going to leave it until tomorrow but the forecast is rain so I thought I'd better get it done. It's looking good, and much less effort not having to stop and empty the grass box every few minutes. And less bending too, which is a bonus for my ever-expanding midriff.

While I was doing that, M was clearing a space in the heated greenhouse for me to install my tomato growing system. It's a long deep plastic trough, with a lid which has four holes. Into each hole goes a wick which reaches up into a large square pot filled with compost, so once the trough is full of water the plants take up as much moisture as they need through the wick. I wonder whether it would work with beer? Can I just sit back and have it delivered intravenously? I think I might set up an experimental system in my shed.

The water now has 24 hours to get up to temperature, and the plan is to plant out my two tomato plants into two of the pots tomorrow. The third pot is reserved for another tomato which is on order, and I've generously donated the fourth one to M, to plant whatever she wants. She's growing various fruits and veg from seed, including aubergines, cucumbers and courgettes, but she says she's always thinking of me, so she's decided to plant an ugli fruit.

Exciting news from the Gardener's World programme - Monty has a new dog! He already has two Labradors, Nigel and Nellie, and now he has a Yorkshire Terrier puppy called Patty. I'm beginning to think M doesn't watch that show for gardening advice at all. She's always had a soft spot for a lovable creature with big sad eyes, and she likes his dogs too.

No popmaster today, but I do have The Times crossword, so that will keep my brain exercised until at least Tuesday.

45

⁓

Social Distancing Diary – Day 42, a day of early morning exercise

A change of routine this Sunday morning, just to break the monotony. I was first up today, fed El Gato and brought M a cup of tea in bed, then surprised her – and myself - by suggesting a long walk before breakfast. The reason is that I've been feeling guilty about overeating and not exercising as much as I should. Yesterday, for example, I had a big breakfast, a huge lunch and a large dinner, punctuated all day long by frequent visits to the biscuit tin. And no exercise apart from my morning walk and cutting the grass. In fact I felt so bloated that I didn't even fancy a Saturday beer, which is unheard of.

It was a lovely morning and the forecast was rain, so we set off on the six-mile circuit at 7am. It's by far the best time of day, you can walk for miles and meet hardly anyone. Today we met only one neighbour and two cyclists during a two-hour walk. No horse riders, no dog walkers and no sweaty joggers. I'm always wary of joggers, I wonder if two metres is far enough away to escape their emissions. I imagine them leaving a trail of steam behind them, like a jet. Or, in my case, a jumbo jet.

When we got home from the walk I had only a small bowl of cereal for breakfast, plus one cup of tea, so felt able to settle down with the Sunday papers feeling very virtuous. An hour later I was weak from hunger. Fortunately, just before I expired, our lovely neighbour popped a batch of fresh scones on the wall for us. And, well, a wee scone doesn't count as snacking, does it? Even with butter and jam, and squirty cream?

We have a great variety of birds of prey around here, including buzzards and red kites. Small animals live in constant danger of being pounced on and eaten. Maybe I better rethink my "no-snacking" policy in case I lose too much weight and a golden eagle swoops on me and carries me away.

The two tomato plants have been installed in their permanent home. I gave them a good soaking then popped them into their big pot in M's greenhouse. Her greenhouse is bursting with trays of seedlings because she's been sowing so many flower and vegetable seeds during lockdown. And they're all growing nicely because she's been able to give them lots of extra attention, which they wouldn't normally get when she's at work Monday to Friday.

I've suggested that this might give her a taste for retirement, but she says she's not ready to retire just yet. I suspect that living with me seven days a week during lockdown is one thing, but making it a permanent arrangement would be a bridge too far.

Also, because she's spending so much time in her greenhouse, there's no room in there for me. She says we'll need to work out an access plan for me to visit my tomatoes. Like parental access, I will have visiting rights once a day, at times to be agreed. And if there's any dispute I expect we'll have to hire a solicitor to sort it out. Or maybe a greengrocer.

As expected, it rained this afternoon, for the first time in a couple of weeks. This will help the grass to grow, which isn't exactly good news. But it might just spur the potatoes to sprout through the ground, which would be a welcome sight. If it wasn't for the record in my diaries I would be beginning to doubt that I'd ever planted them.

And that's the weekend over, tomorrow we start a whole new week. I can hardly contain my excitement.

46

～

Social Distancing Diary – Day 43, a day of prüfungen? Keine prüfungen!

Today was supposed to be the first day of the exams in Scottish schools. So instead of pulling on my walking boots first thing, I should have been slipping into my invigilating shoes. Yes, we have special shoes for invigilating – comfortable so that we can stand in them all day, polished so as to command respect from the pupils, and soft soles so we can creep up behind the little rascals and catch them cheating.

Not that cheating ever happens in MY school, of course. But we hear stories from other invigilators about kids smuggling in their mobile phones disguised as calculators, having facts and figures written on their arms or even feigning injury and hiding notes under bandages. That's why the life of an invigilator is a repetitive one, patrolling up and down between the rows of desks like a POW camp guard patrolling the perimeter fence. Sadly we're not allowed to bring in an Alsatian dog to help us detect potential escapees.

To start us off this year we were due to have German (all levels) and Higher PE today. We have robust measures in place to make sure that kids don't inadvertently turn up for the wrong exam. And it's just as well. Imagine the confusion if any of today's PE and German candidates got mixed up. Instead of describing how the thigh muscles interact with the musculoskeletal system, they'd be confronted with terms like oberschenkelmuskeln and bewegungsapparat. That's one SQA report I'd hate to have to type up.

Popmaster was slightly different today, Ken Bruce is absent from duty and Garry Davies is standing in. Doesn't make the questions any easier, though. I'm glad the first round contestant chose "hits of the 70s" as his bonus topic, at least I had a chance of being able to answer some of the questions. Sometimes being a baby boomer is a good thing.

Just when I thought that the list of cancelled events was complete, it's now been announced that the Royal National Mòd has been called off for 2020. Overseas readers may need to google "Royal National Mòd", but Scots, especially Highland Scots, will understand. It's a great festival of Gaelic culture, music and song and has an undeserved reputation as a hard-drinking event. There's a common misconception that Gaelic singers drink a lot, hence the Mòd's common description in some sections of the press as the "Whisky Olympics".

But whisky production is one of Scotland's major industries, so really all we're doing is supporting the national economy, and we deserve a reward. I'll just have a little water with my reward, thanks.

I'm a veteran of many Mòds, both as a participant and a spectator. It had been due to be held in Inverness this year, which is not far from here, and I feel sorry for all my friends who had been planning to take part. But every cloud has a silver lining. You can have a year off from learning complicated Gaelic songs, you can save some money on hotel bills and your liver can have an extra year to recover, and to build up some resistance for 2021.

In preparation for this week's Thursday Quiz with M Junior and pals, I've been raking in the attic. Not for an encyclopedia to swot up with, but for props to allow me to adopt the guise of a "figure from history", which is this week's theme. I'm happy to say I've found a couple of items which fit the bill admirably, but need a little embellishment, so for the second week in a row I've reverted to being arty and crafty in my shed. With the cardboard and the paint, and the sticky-backed plastic.

No clues right now, but all will be revealed on Thursday night.

Popmaster score: Round 1 – 12 points Round 2 – 6 points

47

～

Social Distancing Diary – Day 44, a day of junk mail

Got excited when I heard the postie this morning. There was a resounding *thump* on the doormat, obviously something important had been delivered! It turned out that everything was addressed to M, nothing for me. That's bad news because it means nobody likes me enough to write to me. But it's good news because it means I don't owe anybody any money.

Nowadays there aren't any bills in the mail anyway, everything comes in by email. Phone bills, credit card bills, car tax, it's all done online. Used to be a time when you could fall behind with your payments and say "they got lost in the post" but that doesn't cut any ice now. I wonder whether the old excuse "the dog ate my homework", could be brought up to date. I will try this one: "Dear bank manager, the dog ate my computer so I couldn't pay off my overdraft".

Anyway, M's mail was a mixture of catalogues and junk. Another catalogue from Atlas For Men, following on from her recent purchase of a pair of elasticated-waist jeans for me. They've obviously worked out she's married to a compulsive eater and they're hoping that as I expand, she will have to order ever larger garments for me.

Also a catalogue from a garden supplies company. It's a very comprehensive one, containing fruit, veg, flowers and tools. Even garden ornaments, including the inevitable gnomes. These gnomes are fairly innocent and quite cute, one with a flower and one with a watering can. Not like some I've seen in other catalogues – there's a very rude one that I'm sure we've all seen. We daren't have that one in our garden. If the neighbours spotted a little old man in need of a haircut baring his bottom towards them, I expect the Police would swiftly arrive. And I don't mean the 70s rock band.

And the final item in the mail was an appeal from the Cats Protection League. We don't know where they got our address from, the only explanation I can think of is that perhaps El Gato put our name down. We knew he was a smart cat put we didn't know he could read and write.

Still no refund from easyJet for my cancelled trip to London in May for the Chelsea Flower Show. I've continued calling their helpline and I get either an engaged tone, or a voice telling me they're too busy, and to call back later. I do appreciate the difficulties they're facing, but wouldn't it be easier for them to make it possible to claim refunds online? I suspect they're deliberately making it difficult in the hope that customers will get fed up trying, and give up. Not this customer, Stelios. According to the financial papers your personal wealth is estimated at around 1.3

billion US dollars. Surely you can spare a few quid for a poor Scottish pensioner?

Their best offer so far is a voucher for a flight to any destination within Europe, valid for the next twelve months. The problem with that is that I don't imagine anyone will be flying anywhere until towards the end of this year, and on December 31 the UK will be out of the EU so there might be visa issues for travellers. And waving an easyJet voucher in the face of some supercilious anti-Brit European border guard will result in me being put on the next flight home, if I'm lucky. And handcuffed by the gendarmerie if I'm not. And I'd better refrain from doing any Inspector Clouseau impressions. "Do you 'ave a rheum pour moi?" "Non Monsieur, but we 'ave a cell. Mind your fingeurs". Clang!

Do they still use the guillotine in France? That would certainly take care of my haircut problem.

Popmaster score: Round 1 – 9 points Round 2 – 9 points

48

～

**Social Distancing Diary – Day 44, a day of Popmaster
success**

Another delivery from the garden supplier today. Twelve begonia plants and a packet of carrot seeds. M took charge of the begonias, tenderly lifting them out of their box and settling them in to her greenhouse to allow them to recover from their long journey. They look remarkably healthy and will soon be able to be potted on. Meantime I got busy in the veg patch, planted the maincrop potatoes and sowed half a packet of carrot seeds. I've kept the other half packet for next year, and have put them away in a safe place. No doubt I'll have trouble next year remembering where I put them, but I hope I find them before the mice do.

And I do believe that, at last, the first potatoes I planted are making an appearance! There's just a hint of a leaf poking through the ground every few inches - and in a straight row - so it's either my early tatties or a very well disciplined row of weeds.

Massive success in Popmaster today, the bonus topic was

"Bond themes of the 1960s" which was right up my street. As a teenager I was a huge James Bond fan, read all the books and saw all the films. It wasn't easy seeing films when I was growing up, our nearest village had no cinema, the only movies available were shown in the village hall. A crowd of us thought nothing of walking eight miles each way on a Saturday, just to see the latest blockbuster, which was probably "Lassie Come Home". All that way to see a collie dog. Considering we were surrounded by sheep farms, we could have saved ourselves a walk.

I see Boris has become a daddy. Again. He's just come back to work after his sick leave, and now I suppose he'll be applying to go on paternity leave. Who signs his leave applications? The Queen? Is she not too busy signing birthday cards for centenarians, now that we're all living longer?

I've always hated our vacuum cleaner. It's a Dyson, so quite an expensive one, and we've had it a long time, but it and I have had issues from Day 1. It's one of those round ones which is supposed to follow you everywhere like a big ball, but whenever I try to pull it round a corner it always falls over on its side and lies there like a helpless puppy wanting to be picked up. I've been trying for years to invent an excuse to get rid of it, but M has always defended it and blamed me for not being able to control it. Control it? I'd rather try to control a toddler having a meltdown in a supermarket aisle.

Finally the perfect excuse has presented itself. After her recent spell of painting everything, in every room, from every angle, M has realised that there's a danger the Hoover from Hell will rub against her nice glossy skirting boards and mark them. And indeed, examination of the ball-shaped cylinder reveals white paint marks on its sides from years of failing to follow me round corners. So at last we've decided to upgrade it to a modern, upright, cordless one which won't need to be dragged around the house like a reluctant dog being taken to the vet.

I was able to order online, even though the prices made my eyes water, and through the tears I picked the first available delivery slot, which was tonight between 7 and 11pm. Sure enough, a text message arrived: "your delivery is 0 minutes away". I wondered why the message was accompanied by menacing music, but when the package arrived I remembered I'd ordered a Shark.

Popmaster score: Round 1 – 27 points Round 2 – 9 points

49

⌇

Social Distancing Diary – Day 46, a day of memory loss

It's happened again! Once again lockdown has lost me a day. Observant readers will have noticed that yesterday was Day 44, and the day before was also Day 44. All of a sudden it's Day 46 so where's my missing day? Did I fall asleep for 24 hours? Did I do anything? Should I add amnesia to my list of ailments along with gluttony, idleness and lethargy? Did my massive Popmaster score finally tip me over the edge?

This has happened twice now. My only excuse is the sheer repetitiveness of lockdown, with every day feeling just like the previous one, even at what used to be weekends. But at my age I can't afford to lose any days so I'd better start concentrating. Perhaps it's just as well the exams have been cancelled, I'd probably be standing in front of a Physics class right now, wishing them luck in Gaelic.

My memory is getting so bad, I've almost forgotten what a dream ring tastes like. There's some light on the horizon though, as Inverness-based baker Harry Gow has begun reopening some of his shops. He started with one of his Inverness shops, as you might expect, but I was excited to hear he was planning to expand into Ross-shire. My excitement was crushed yesterday when he announced that his Ross-shire expansion is starting with Alness and Tain, not Dingwall. Come on Harry, your number one fan is here with his tongue hanging out.

The Shark, which arrived last night, has had its batteries charged and been tested. It's light, manoeuvrable and obedient, nothing at all like its predecessor. Nothing at all like its owner either, come to think of it.

No cable, so the skirting boards are immune from damage, a claimed forty minutes of runtime between charges, and folds up neatly for storage. No indicators, but it does have a set of headlamps. I have to dip them when I meet M coming the other way.

Congratulations to NHS fundraising hero Captain Tom, on reaching his 100th birthday today. For my overseas readers who might not know - Captain Tom Moore, a 99-year-old WW2 veteran who walks with the aid of a zimmer frame, set out to walk 100 laps of his garden to raise £1000 for the National Health Service. He's now approaching 200 laps and has raised an amazing £30 million. He's now been recognised as a national hero and been promoted to Honorary Colonel.

Makes me feel a right wuss for girning about a sore ankle. Overseas readers may need to google "wuss" and "girning".

Thursday night is Zoom quiz night. With the historical dressing-up theme. I transformed myself into Napoleon with the aid of an old hat I found in the attic and a red white and blue rosette made from an old cereal box and some poster paints. It's quite effective but very tight and uncomfortable. Napoleon was famous for being short tempered. If his hat was as tight as mine I'm not surprised.

He was also famous for not being tall. I think the politically correct term is "vertically challenged". In fact he's described as short, ill-tempered and domineering. Remind you of anyone?

The real Napoleon managed to come second at Waterloo. What did I achieve in the weekly quiz? A miserable third. Out of three.

Next week's theme: movie stars. Stand by attic, here I come.

Popmaster score: Round 1 – 9 points Round 2 – 15 points

50

Social Distancing Diary – Day 47, a day of failed negotiations

Today is Friday May 1, and I was rudely awakened by M pinching and punching me and triumphantly proclaiming: "Pinch, punch, first of the month!" Yet again, I lose.

I should have been up at dawn, washing my face in the morning dew. According to legend, that's supposed to make you beautiful, but I've never done it. Now I fear I may have left it too late.

El Gato has been missing for a couple of days. M always puts out food for him just as it's getting dark, after the birds have gone to bed. Or wherever birds go after dark. These past two nights he hasn't appeared so we were imagining he'd gone back to his proper home. Until this morning, at 8.48am, I was throwing out some toast crumbs to the birds and there he was, staring up at me with a "why is my dish empty?" expression on his face.

Some overnight rain has given my early potatoes a boost. They're shooting up through the ground at quite a rate, I can almost see them growing. So I've covered them up with earth to encourage them to keep growing and stop the tubers from turning green. It doesn't work for me, I'm quite used to being kept in the dark and I haven't grown in years. And so far I haven't turned green. Except for a couple of occasions on the Stornoway ferry, the morning after the Mòd.

I've been reading in the papers about some car insurance companies who are giving their customers rebates because their cars are being used much less than usual, therefore the risk of a claim is reduced. Admiral, which is the UK's biggest insurer, has been giving policyholders a nice wee gift of a £25 rebate. Never one to miss out on a freebie, I thought I'd try my luck with my own motor insurer, whom I'd better not name, for fear of legal action.

We are lucky enough to have two cars, our main one (driven by both of us) is being used only once a week for M's shopping trip to Dingwall, around five miles a week. And M has her own car which she uses for commuting to work, and which has done a total of 0 miles since lockdown began. Both cars are insured with the same company, so I thought I had a good case for a payback.

No mention of refunds on the relevant website, so I called their customer helpline and spoke to a very nice lady who told me, very nicely, that they weren't issuing refunds. I suggested to her, also very nicely, that this might well affect my decision when renewal time comes around. This is a veiled threat which has served me well in the past, with various companies. By suggesting taking my business elsewhere I've successfully had my

RAC membership fee slashed, and obtained a reduction and a two-year freeze on my plumbing insurance. Although perhaps "freeze" isn't the best choice of word for a plumbing insurance.

This scenario, however, failed to touch the heart of the Post Office lady. She simply reiterated the "no refunds" policy and said that when renewal is due it will be up to me to decide what to do. I assured her that I have a long memory and will remember this conversation when the time comes.

Which is an absolute lie because I can never remember anything. In fact I wouldn't even be able to remember this morning, if it wasn't for the bruises left behind by the "pinch, punch" brutality.

She was unfailingly polite and we parted as friends, but I'd love to know what she was thinking. Probably something along the lines of: "get yer wallet open, ya miserable tight fisted Scottish skinflint".

Ahoy there, Admiral – I'd like to come aboard, if I like the cut of your jib. And your renewal price.

Popmaster score: Round 1 – 12 points Round 2 – 12 points

51

⌘

Social Distancing Diary – Day 48, a day of long words and long walks

Today is Saturday May 2. I've started including the day and date, because simply recording the day number can lead to confusion. And because every day is a carbon copy of every other day I find it very difficult to keep track of where we are in the calendar. Yesterday I was shocked to find it was the first of May, I thought it was mid-April. Doubly shocked to realise that I'm two weeks older than I thought I was.

I know today is Saturday because when M came home from the shop she brought me The Times. She buys it on Saturdays and Wednesdays because it takes me a couple of days to read it, and usually three days to complete the crossword. The Saturday edition of The Times is massive. Today's issue has 88 pages, plus a "Weekend" supplement and a "Saturday Review" section, and a glossy magazine as well. And I have to confess I sometimes have difficulties understanding the words. Some of them are nearly half an inch long, for goodness sake.

Interesting to see lots of adverts in the papers for holidays in 2021. It's becoming increasingly likely that there will be NO holidays for anyone for the rest of this year, which is disappointing for M and I because we always book our holidays a year in advance. This year we were due to go in October and, while it hasn't actually been cancelled yet, it's looking more and more doubtful that there will be international flights by then. So it looks like we'll be holidaying in the Ross-shire Riviera this year, with maybe a couple of trips to M Junior's B&B in Costa del Farmyard.

And just to rub salt into the wound, I see the Chief Executive of Heathrow Airport has been making predictions about air travel after lockdown. As well as the usual sensible precautions relating to social distancing in airports and pre-flight testing, he's suggesting that Heathrow should be open only for "low risk passengers". Some commentators are taking this to mean the exclusion of vulnerable groups, including the over 65s which, sadly, (and I hate to admit it) includes me.

So if it comes to pass – and it's only speculation at this stage - only young, fit travellers will be permitted to fly and M and I will be excluded. Even though we're both blessed with good health and consider ourselves to be quite fit. I mean, six months ago we climbed an eight and a half thousand foot mountain in Patagonia. Ok, so we started from six and a half thousand feet, but let's not quibble.

Here's a test, Mr CEO – send your passengers on the 6-mile walk with M. Regardless of age, if they can keep up with her they're fit to fly. Try it yourself. And bring your own oxygen, you'll be needing it.

Mixed weather today, sunshine and showers. I had a bit of a lazy day, reading my way through all those papers, while M was out in her greenhouse, potting on some plants. I did manage a long walk in the afternoon though, M set off on the 6-miler - anti clockwise - and I set off in the opposite direction, met her halfway and walked home with her. This is working out well for my ankle, because I walk half the distance at half the speed, and the other half at full speed.

So here's today's exam question: If a man walks three miles out at 2mph and three miles back at 3mph, how much beer does it take to stop him complaining about his ankle?

No Popmaster today, but I got 3 out of 5 in the Daily Mirror Pub Quiz. Which is a vast improvement on yesterday, when I scored 0 as opposed to M, who got 5.

52

Social Distancing Diary – Day 49, a day of rain. And TV violence.

Today is Sunday May 3. I know it's Sunday because M came home from the paper shop with Scotland on Sunday. Another day, another crossword, but not nearly as challenging as The Times one.

Up early, fed El Gato, brought M tea in bed. Just a repeat of last Sunday, really. Had a nice dry walk and only met one dog walker. I've met her several times since lockdown started, she has a black dog with staring eyes who looks quite aggressive and the first time we met he came running towards me, so I mentally christened him "Angry Dog". I asked her if he was friendly. She just kind of shrugged, so I took that as a "no". M does the same when people ask about me.

However, every time we met the dog would come bounding towards me so I thought that maybe he's not aggressive, just trying to be friendly, so I started giving him a wee treat. I always have a bag of treats in my pocket because I have several doggy pals whom I often meet. Anyway, Angry Dog accepted his treat gratefully, and now every time he sees me he comes running, sits nicely, and takes his treat gently. Today he abandoned his owner and came running to me from a long way behind. I would do exactly the same if I saw Harry Gow in front of me with a pocket full of dream rings.

I was lucky it stayed dry for my walk, because soon after I got home the rain started. Nasty drizzly rain, the type that makes you wetter than heavy rain does. Very good for the garden, though. As long as it remembers to stop. So it was a day for staying indoors, and on a normal Sunday there would be motorbike racing on telly but of course that's all cancelled so there's nothing much to watch. So I've downloaded a box set everyone's been raving about. It's called The Sopranos.

After twenty-five years singing in choirs I thought I knew a thing or two about sopranos. Boy did I get that wrong! I've watched two episodes so far and there hasn't been much harmony. There's been nothing but stabbings, shootings and stranglings. And that's just within their own family, you should see what they do to their enemies. These guys are even more badly behaved than the Gaelic choir sopranos at the Mòd, and that's saying something.

Tomorrow we enter week number seven of lockdown. I went into isolation a week before lockdown started, so that means it's nearly eight weeks since I wore proper, smart, presentable clothes. I've been slobbing around in polo shirts, micro fleeces and activity trousers (although there isn't usually much activity!) every day. I said to M that I'd really like to wear a nice smart shirt, a jacket, dress trousers and nice shoes, just for a change. And also that I'd love to get away from home, just for a change of scene.

Her response was that I should dress up smartly as if I was going to town, with neatly pressed trousers and polished shoes. And I should walk around the garden dressed like that, making sure everyone sees me. Then, she says, some men in white coats will come and take me away, and I'll get a change of scene all right.

Finished off the day with a phone call to M Junior, who tells me that this week's Zoom quiz theme has changed from "movie star" to "masquerade", so I need to design and make a mask. Better get stuck into the Crunchy Nut Corn Flakes tomorrow – I'm gonna need a cereal box.

53

ᔕᔕ

Social Distancing Diary – Day 50, a day of sore fingers

Today is Monday May 4. I imagine we've all had enough of seeing "may the 4th be with you" popping up in our Facebook feeds along with images of Darth Vader. In East Scotland of course it's "may the Forth be with you" along with an image of Sean Connery.

Traditionally, today is a bank holiday. The first Monday in May was always a day off school, a day off work and a day for relaxing. This year is different in two ways. Firstly, for many people, and for all us oldies, every day is like that right now, so how would we know the difference? And secondly, this year's May-day bank holiday has been moved to Friday May 8, to celebrate the anniversary of VE Day, the end of the Second World War in Europe. Today's papers are full of commemorative photos of Churchill and his famous V sign. I tried following his example and giving a V sign to everyone I see, but instead of ending WW2 it appears to be starting WW3. Some people have no sense of humour.

So, instead of being a school closure day, it was planned for exams to take place throughout Scotland today. And today's was supposed to be Higher and Advanced Higher English, which is one of the biggest exams in terms of candidates. In my school we would have had a couple of hundred anxious souls quivering outside the exam room, waiting to start, desperately trying to remember how to spell "desperately", the rules of grammar, quotes from Shakespeare and whether I really does come before E except after C. Or, as my Yorkshire granny would have said: "Aye before Eee".

The only Shakespeare quote I remember from school is "If music be the food of love, I'll have the Meat Loaf followed by Banarama, and the Spice Girls". At least that's how I remember it.

And so to gardening. After yesterday's drizzle, today was lovely, warm and dry. The postie brought some more plants for M this morning, begonias, cucumber and courgette mini plants. She retired to her greenhouse to sort them out and plant them into their proper containers and she looked so busy, I felt guilty doing nothing. So I carried on doing just that until after Popmaster.

Then I thought I'd better do something in the garden. Just to pass a couple of hours before lunch. When we moved to this house more than twenty years ago, we embarked on a revamp of the garden. One of our innovations was to plant a border of mixed shrubs along one perimeter, to give us a little privacy and to hide the wire fence which separates us from the public footpath running alongside. Another reason was to keep cats out and dogs in, and we all know how that worked out, don't we?

All of the shrubs have thrived and are now substantial, mature bushes, but one of the problems is that weeds and grasses persist in growing at the base of the bushes, and has to be weeded by hand every couple of years. So I dug out a kneeling stool, a hand fork and a pair of gloves and set to. All went quite well until I came to the Berberis. The gardeners amongst you will recognise the name Berberis, its common name is Barberry and it's best known for producing very sharp spikes. Our variety is Berberis Darwinii, named after Charles Darwin, and quite honestly I wish he'd never discovered it, far less brought it home.

Even through the stout gardening gloves I was wearing, every time I reached under the bush to pull out some grass my hands were spiked mercilessly by these needle-sharp prongs. By the time I was finished my hands were so punctured I had to be excused from washing the dishes.

I wonder how long I can keep this excuse running?

Popmaster score: Round 1 – 3 points Round 2 – 12 points

54

∽

Social Distancing Diary – Day 51, a day of seeing the fragrant Joanna

Today is Tuesday May 5. Frosty start to the day, morning walk was bright and brisk. And I met a new animal – a nice black and white cat who was very friendly, he came to see me and allowed me to stroke him. Unlike El Gato, who refuses to get close and only tolerates us because he sees us as a source of food.

Then I met the usual crop of dogs, including Angry Dog, who's rapidly becoming my best pal. Sadly, I suspect he too sees me solely as a source of food. It's very much a "take, take, take" and no "give" relationship with these animals. I have a similar relationship with the fridge.

Excited to see a couple of photos in today's Daily Mail – yes it's the absolutely fabulous Joanna Lumley! Haven't seen her on telly for ages, but here she was, queuing at her local supermarket in Battersea. And, being the trouper she is, she was happy to pose for selfies with her fellow shoppers.

Imagine being so famous that people want to be photographed beside you. I'm old enough to remember street photographers who sometimes used to carry a wee monkey to sit on your shoulder for a photo. Alas, I fear that today, the monkey would take one look at my wild hairstyle and refuse to come anywhere near me.

I've always associated Battersea with the power station and the dog's home, but now I know about Sainsbury's supermarket and its glamorous customer it's suddenly become a lot more attractive. As soon as this lockdown is lifted I shall volunteer to do the shopping for M. "I'm just popping out to Sainsbury's in Battersea dear, I may be some time..."

I've had a very welcome email from the SQA (that's the Scottish Qualifications Authority, for my foreign readers). They've realised that we Chief Invigilators do a huge amount of preparatory work in advance of the exams, and because of this year's cancellations all that work is wasted, and, more importantly, unpaid. I remember at the time of cancellation my lovely SQA Co-ordinator contacted the SQA to ask about payment for this work, and the answer was: "if they don't cover the exams, they don't get paid". And I've been composing an angry letter in my head ever since. Luckily it was still at the planning stage.

Now there appears to have been a rethink, and the email includes a claim form for any hours I have spent in preparation. So I've filled it in and sent it back, and we'll wait and see if they just pay out, or if they quibble about it. But even if they pay it out in full, I don't expect a life-changing amount. The rate of pay is pretty basic, as you might expect from a public body, and of course the tax man takes his cut before it even reaches me, so don't expect any social distancing diaries from Richard Branson's island just yet.

My final six tomato plants arrived today. The variety is Shirley and they're "mini plugs", which doesn't mean they're tiny bathroom basin accessories, although they would do the job nicely. Today they're spending the day in the spare bedroom, getting used to not being thrown around in the back of a delivery van, and tomorrow I'll have to decide where they're going to live permanently. Initially they'll be applying for visas to go into M's greenhouse, because that's the one with the heater. Temperatures were down to zero last night, so the plants were very grateful for the warmth. I hope they repay this investment by fruiting abundantly.

Finishing the day off sticking some new photos into my scrapbook. Now where's the scissors? And the Daily Mail? And which page is Joanna on?

Popmaster score: Round 1 – 6 points Round 2 – 6 points

55

⌇

Social Distancing Diary – Day 52, a day of fine dining

Today is Wednesday May 6. A touch of frost again last night, but a beautiful morning for my walk.

M shocked me this morning by bring home what I thought was a plastic box full of wee speckled stones. She told me: "I saw the fish van when I was going to the shop, and I bought these, just for a change". Well, a meal of wee stones would certainly be a change. And how long do you boil them for? I have very few teeth left anyway, and that would surely finish them off.

Just as I was about to have her certified insane, M explained that they weren't stones, but were in fact quail's eggs. Quail's eggs? From the fish van? Evidently so. Perhaps because of lockdown regulations quails aren't supposed to socialise with each other, so they've been reclassified as fish so that they can keep on laying their eggs.

Anyway, I've never tasted a quail's egg in my life. My idea of fine dining is eating beans from a plate, not cold from the tin, and stirring my tea with a teaspoon instead of a screwdriver, but because M is an avid fan of BBC's "Masterchef" she is well acquainted with the concept, and knows exactly how to cook quail's eggs so we had some for lunch. After one minute, they were perfectly hard-boiled, just like snack-sized hen's eggs. Or like those mini-eggs you get inside your Easter egg, but with less chocolate.

The difficulty was shelling them. The shells are very thin and delicate, and impossible to remove except in tiny little fragments. M, having watched the process on telly, soon developed a system which involved rolling gently (the egg, not herself) and peeling off the shell in large sections. I, on the other hand, found this too delicate an operation and was forced to pick miniscule pieces of shell. By the time M had shelled a dozen I had managed one and a half. They were tasty, though, with rich orange yolks. We have fourteen left for tomorrow. Better start practising my shelling technique now.

Progress (of a sort) at last from easyJet. Finally managed to work out how to apply for a refund. It's not easy to find on their website, but they helpfully sent me an email with a link to their "covid-19" help page and there, buried at the very bottom in tiny print, was the refund procedure. I've come to a compromise with them. I had return flights booked for M and me to go to London in a couple of weeks, so what I've done is rebooked my own flight for a future event in London next year and asked for a refund for M's flight. And before you ask, no I'm not sneaking off to London to stalk Joanna Lumley, although now that you mention it.....

And after applying for the refund, I got an email back from

easyJet acknowledging my application and telling me they're working on it. Well that was reassuring. Not quite so reassuring was the advice that if I hadn't received the refund after a certain period I should get in touch with them. And the "certain period"? Ninety days! Yes, NINETY DAYS! Phileas Fogg went around the world in eighty days, and that was in 1872, before the Kessock Bridge was opened.

But if we're still in isolation in 90 days it will be Day 142 of social distancing diaries so I shall update you then.

Popmaster score: Round 1 – 9 points Round 2 – 15 points

56

∾

Social Distancing Diary – Day 53, a day of strenuous activity

Today is Thursday May 7. Yet another fine day, and a pleasant morning walk apart from a minor traffic jam in the woods. Just as I met a man and his dog, a cyclist came up behind me so we had three people and a dog trying to share a two-person wide path. With all the agility of a young gazelle I sprang off the track into the woods to leave the path clear for the two of them to pass safely. Well I say young gazelle, but perhaps elderly rhino might be more accurate.

Last winter was the wettest in the twenty years since we came to live in this house, and a large part of the garden spent the winter under water. I wouldn't dignify it with the title "lawn" so let's just think of it as a grassy area. Of course, now that the floods have subsided it's a mossy area so something needed to be done. By me. Oh joy.

Fortuitously, M had a Zoom meeting with her school colleagues this morning, and needed to be left alone without interference from me, so I took myself out and tackled the situation. I have a packet of grass seed left over from last year, or maybe the year before, so I thought that if I rake the moss away and expose the soil underneath, I can simply re-seed the mossy area. Have you tried raking moss? Phew it's an arduous task, more strenuous than any of the celebrity keep-fit workouts currently trending on YouTube. I should have filmed it, and become the latest online health and exercise guru. I could call it "glowing with the gardener", or, more accurately, "sweating with Sandy".

It looks easy when Monty Don does it, but maybe he just does a little bit then gets his assistants to do the hard work off-camera. Unfortunately my assistant was ensconced with her zoomie pals so I had to do it all by myself. Within a short time I had amassed barrowload after barrowload of moss which I had to cram into the garden recycling bin, and which will have to wait until two weeks from today to get emptied. The garden bin and I went into isolation at the same time, and I'm jealous of it for getting out first.

Meanwhile, M's Zoom meeting seemed to go quite well. I waited with her just to make sure everything was working, in case my amazing ICT skills might be required. Even though Zoom hadn't been invented when I passed my ECDL exams, I can still resolve any problems. I'll let you into the secret. Switch off, count to ten, and switch on again. There you go, that will save you a fortune in computer repair bills.

And immediately after her meeting M headed off to Dingwall for her weekly shopping trip. As usual, she was able to get almost everything on her list including (hurrah!) beer but not including (boo!) a dream ring. Come on Harry, get your Dingwall shop open plccccasc.

Tonight was our weekly Zoom quiz, with M Junior plus two pals and me. You will remember this week's theme was "masquerade" so I needed to make/obtain a mask. Well, I have to confess I cheated. I found a site on the internet which had mask templates ready to print and cut out, so I did just that, and glued it on to an old cereal box. I chose one with an owl's face, which I thought would lend me an air of wisdom. And did it work? No, I came last. Again.

Next week it's my turn to host the quiz, so I've chosen "movie characters" as my theme. Simply because that was the original theme for this week and I'd already begun preparing my props. Can't tell you who I'm going to be, of course, but I can assure you it won't be anyone slim. Or well groomed.

Popmaster score: Round 1 – 15 points Round 2 – 12 points

57

~

Social Distancing Diary – Day 54, a day of blind faith

Today is Friday May 8. Also the 75th anniversary of VE Day, this is the Mayday bank holiday we always have on the first Monday in May, but this year we're having it on Friday. And just to confuse me even further, M and I went on a walk together (yes, I know!) this morning and we were halfway through it when I remarked how quiet it was for a Saturday morning and she had to correct me and tell me it's Friday. How is anyone meant to keep track of the days/weeks/months?

Readers who have been with me since the early days of this diary might remember Days 18 and 19, and the saga of the vertical blinds. I had to bodge a repair to make up for some missing parts, just to keep the kitchen blinds operating until a new, made to measure, set arrived. Well, yesterday a parcel delivery man dropped off a small package on the doorstep and when we opened it we found the slats for the blinds, but not the rail to hang them from. I was just about to phone the blind manufacturer in full Mr Angry mode, when I read the label and saw that it said: "package 1 of 2".

Sure enough, today the same van arrived and dropped off a long slim parcel, marked "package 2 of 2", so my delivery is now complete. That's the good news. The bad news, of course, is that the new blinds had to be fitted. And the big question upon everyone's mind was – would they fit?

So it was with some trepidation that I unpacked the parcels and held the new top rail up against the window to see if it was the right length. But, thanks to my careful measuring on Day 19 it was exactly the right size. Thank goodness I listened to my old woodwork teacher when he hammered into us the motto: "measure twice, cut once". It's fairly evident from my exam results that he was the only teacher I listened to.

Actually, I tend to take it to extremes, and measure many times, especially these days when everything is measured using the metric system. Ask me to estimate a two foot length of four by two and I'm pretty accurate, but visualise 100 millimetres? Not a clue, pass the measuring tape!

And the blind fitted without too much hassle, or inappropriate language. However I needed M to help install the top rail. That's the trouble when you have a window that's five feet wide and your own wingspan is only four feet six inches.

Remember I told you yesterday about raking moss with a view to reseeding a couple of patches of lawn? Well today was mild and slightly damp, perfect weather for grass seed to germinate, so I collected my one-(possibly two, or maybe three)-year-old grass seed from the shed and sprinkled it liberally over both areas. Then I returned to the shed to fetch a rake, just to press the seed into the ground, and by the time I returned – no more than a minute later – the whole patch was black with birds pecking up my precious grass seed. We feed these birds so much and this is how they repay me?

Drastic measures were called for, so I found a couple of protective garden fleece shrouds which were last used to protect sweetcorn (again from birds!) in the garden a few years ago. The material allows rain and light to get in, but keeps feathered pests out, so I've pegged them in position and will leave them there until the seeds germinate. Hopefully no more than a few days, if this weather keeps up.

Meantime, the blackbirds will have to subsist on breadcrumbs, apples and highly expensive wild bird seed bought from the classiest shop in Dingwall. Poundstretcher.

Popmaster score: Round 1 – 6 points Round 2 – 15 points

58

Social Distancing Diary – Day 55, a day of pink nostalgia

Today is Saturday May 9, and when I awoke it was warm and wet. And it was just as bad out of bed. After yesterday's accidental walk with M (when I thought it was Saturday) I had to go on the real Saturday one this morning. And again in the afternoon, for six miles. In the rain.

Got soaked both times. I'll be really annoyed if I avoid covid-19 only to catch pneumonia.

M gets regular supplies of clothing catalogues. Every time she buys something from a supplier, that supplier starts bombarding her with catalogues in the hope that she'll become a regular customer. Usually, I like to buy my clothes in a shop, so that I can feel the quality and try them on. Especially trousers, because I'm rather short in the leg. And we won't mention waist size.

Shirts, however, are usually safe to buy by mail order. And while M was browsing in the catalogue of one of her favourite suppliers I just happened to look over her shoulder and saw a very nice range of shirts. I think you'd classify them as "smart but casual" which is good in one way because you're not expected to wear a tie, but not so good because they generally need ironed. Unless you wear them under a jumper, which kind of defeats the purpose.

But the thing that caught my eye was the colour. I'm very partial to a pink shirt, and since I lost my favourite one a few years ago I'm always on the lookout for a replacement. We were on holiday in Venice one summer, and it was very warm indeed. So much so that it was necessary to change shirts more than once a day (unlike, in Scotland, once a month) and I had got into the habit of washing my shirts in the hotel room and hanging them outside the window, where they would dry overnight. And our room was on the top floor so there was no danger of some passing gondolier reaching across with his oar and stealing my shirt. Because they do that, you know.

There was another risk, however. In summer there's a danger of thunderstorms sweeping down from the Dolomite mountains and battering Venice, and M being a regular weather watcher advised me not to leave my shirts out overnight, just in case. Did I listen? What do you think?

My very favourite pink shirt was on a hanger, outside the window, when we went to bed. In the morning the hanger was gone, and so was the shirt. Anguished, I rushed downstairs, much to the bemusement of the cleaning lady, and ran along the canal banks in both directions but there was no sign of either hanger or shirt. And no pink-shirted residents either, although I spent the rest of our trip staring suspiciously at every gondolier

I saw. M and I still often talk about that incident. Well, she talks and I listen. Which I wish I'd done that day.

And ever since then I've been searching for a replacement, and bought quite a few pink shirts over the years but never found one to match it. This one in M's catalogue looked rather nice though, and after dropping some very hefty hints she took pity on me and ordered it. And now a nice parcel delivery man has delivered it. And it's just as nice in the flesh as it looked in the catalogue so it's hanging in the wardrobe waiting for an occasion where I can wear it.

Judging from the news in today's papers it might be waiting some considerable time. I hear Boris is going to announce some easing of lockdown in England, but here in Scotland it looks like we're going to stay isolated for some time yet. So I'm going to remain stuck within these same four walls. Which are beautifully decorated by the way, dear, in case you're reading this.

Maybe I should move out to the shed for a week or two, just for a change of scene. And if you're passing and see a pink shirt hanging out of the shed window please just leave it alone.

59

Social Distancing Diary – Day 56, a day of stress relief

Today is Sunday May 10. Much colder this morning, but we had a dry walk. Later, it began to snow so it looks like winter is dealing us a final blow before giving way to warmer weather. My carrots haven't come through the ground yet, so any snowman I might make will have to be noseless. I suppose the politically correct term will be "nasally challenged".

I've had to earth up my potatoes even further, they're really taking a growth spurt but I need to make sure they don't get affected by frost. The Blessed Monty covers his up with straw, which I think is rather messy, and he even recommends using grass clippings which would surely lead to a major weed problem later in the season. One of my neighbours has a wooden frame covered with bubble wrap, which is quite a good idea, but whenever I get any bubble wrap I can't resist popping it, so that idea isn't going to work for me. Yes I know, popping bubble wrap is a very immature thing to do, but it's very addictive.

And actually it has been proved to be a stress reliever so any time I'm angered about what I read in the papers or see on the telly I always feel the need to do some popping. And depending on the level of my anger you might hear anything from an occasional single "pop" to a full-blown machine gun effect, reminiscent of Al Capone and his gang robbing the Bank of Chicago.

Speaking of gang culture, I must say I'm now addicted to The Sopranos. I'm still watching series 1 and have reached the penultimate episode so I guess I'll be downloading series 2 before too long. I never expected to enjoy it quite so much, I just thought I'd give it a try because of all the glowing reviews it gets, but now I've been drawn in to the backstabbing, double dealing and outright violence of everyday life in the mafia. It's almost as good as a Friday night in Dingwall. Pre-lockdown, of course.

I have a new creature to tell you about. Well, he's actually not new at all, he's been visiting us for a few years now, and in spite of being chased with oaths, threats and angry shouts he persists in coming several times a day. He's a big black crow who has, up until now, been nameless. He perches in a neighbouring tree from where he can see whether it's safe to descend upon our back garden and steal the bread M puts out for the smaller birds. Because of this perching habit she's decreed that he will be known as Percy.

And Percy is very persistent indeed. He doesn't only steal the birds' bread, he also has a habit of clinging on to one of the nut feeders and swinging wildly in an attempt to knock it to the ground.

And when we chase him he doesn't fly far away like the seagulls do, he simply pops up on to his tree and, wiping his beak disdainfully on a branch, sneers down at us with a knowing look that says, in crow language: "...I'll be back..."

This afternoon I excused myself from the long walk on the pretext of resting my ankle. Which I did, whilst watching The Sopranos with a wee cup of tea. And possibly a chocolate biscuit.

And finally, some exciting news! This weekend I've been treated to not one, but TWO viewings of the wonderful Joanna Lumley. Firstly, out of boredom we watched a kid's film on tv called "Gangsta Granny" which featured Joanna as The Queen. And secondly, a couple of my lovely friends have sent me a clip from the BBC VE day programmes which shows Joanna telephoning an elderly lady who served in the Navy during WW2 and arranging for her to be presented with her medals.

It would be worth joining the Navy, just to get a call from the fragrant Joanna, but I suspect I may have left it too late.

60

Social Distancing Diary – Day 57, a day of coffee with friends. At a distance.

Today is Monday May 11. Very cold this morning brrr. We have a weather device which records temperature and it says that it fell to zero last night. Very glad I had the foresight to earth up the tatties yesterday, and switch on the greenhouse heater before bedtime. The weather station thing is very handy. It comes in two parts – one mounted on an arch in the garden which transmits data, and one in the house which receives and displays it. It doesn't only tell us the current situation, it also records minimum and maximum temperatures, percentage humidity, and sunshine levels inside and outside the house.

Well, there aren't actually any sunshine levels inside the house, except for when I light up the room with my dazzling smile. Which only happens when M comes home from her shopping, with my week's supply of beer.

It also tells us the day, month, year and time. Everything you could possibly need, in fact. It even has an alarm clock function, which I don't need. My alarm call every weekday morning is when M brings me a cup of tea in bed before she heads off on her morning walk.

El Gato arrived this morning as usual, ate his breakfast then wandered off. We were worried about him last night because by bedtime he still hadn't appeared, but he seems to be alive and well today. He refuses to tell us where he's been, but we suspect his real family might have had a special Sunday lunch so he stayed at home to share that, rather than come for our offerings of boring old cat food.

He's in the habit now of coming at breakfast time and again at teatime, and disappearing outwith these times. Unlike Percy, who carries out constant raids on the birds' bread throughout the day. If we're standing at the kitchen window he watches us from his tree, and if we move away or turn our backs for a second, down he swoops, quickly grabs a beakful of bread and immediately does a u-turn and lands back on his branch. If the RAF ever need to train their pilots in stealth bombing techniques, all they need do is come here and study Percy's flying skills.

Another batch of scones arrived this morning from my lovely Italian next-door neighbour, which was quite good timing because I was invited to a coffee morning at 11am. Yes, a coffee morning! Not a real one, of course, but a virtual one, run on Zoom with a group of old friends. The original invitation was for 10.30 but that's Popmaster time, so absolutely not suitable for me. Judging by today's scores, however, it might have been better if I'd given Popmaster a miss.

The beauty of virtual coffee mornings is that you can have your scones all to yourself, no sharing is expected, so by 10.55 I was all ready, with scone, butter, jam and a mug of tea. And after one or two wee technical glitches there we were, four of us, seeing and hearing each other for the first time in a couple of months. It was good to catch up with each other's family news and to hear what we've all been up to during lockdown. It was also an opportunity for us all to have a moan about all the things we're missing because of covid-19. In no particular order - holidays, eating out, visiting friends, shopping, dream rings. Guess who came up with that last one?

We chatted for an hour and a half, which took me nicely up to lunchtime, so that meant that my morning looked like this: drink tea – get up – walk – breakfast – drink tea – popmaster – coffee morning – lunch.

You would think that, with an inactive morning like that, I would jump at the chance to accompany M on the afternoon six-mile hike. Well, you'd be wrong.

Popmaster score: Round 1 – 0 points Round 2 – 9 points

61

࿓

Social Distancing Diary – Day 58, a day of spiritual memories

Today is Tuesday May 12. One of the most satisfying things about writing this daily diary is the feedback and comments I get from all of you. Mostly your comments are amusing, supportive and sympathetic, but yesterday I got one which said something along the lines of: "I saw you on the telly last night, singing your wee heart out..." It was a Gaelic programme from a number of years ago - 2005 I think – filmed in a church not too far from here. Good old BBC, saving money by repeating fifteen-year-old shows. Where's my repeat fees? Can I deduct them from my TV licence payment? No, I thought not.

Anyway, when I went on to BBC iplayer there I was. Much younger, better groomed and slim(mer), smartly dressed in kilt and sporran. And they must have been desperately short of soloists, because I'm leading one of the psalms, in Gaelic, with all the power of a top quality Gaelic Choir behind me. And as the minister addressed the congregation, I appear to be sitting, thinking spiritual thoughts. In actual fact I was probably thinking about the spirits in my sporran flask. Glenmorangie, if memory serves me well.

If anyone wants a laugh at my expense, it was on BBC Alba at 6.50pm Sunday May 10.

For some time now I've been planning to have our old garden fence replaced. It's a typical wire fence which runs alongside a public path, and which forms the border containing the berberis (ouch) and other bushes. The fence is almost forty years old, and is worn out, shaky and sagging. And yes, I know how it feels.

So, in order to restore a proper boundary, and to stop Dog F from escaping when she comes to visit, we've decided to have a wooden fence installed. I measured it out last week, and estimated it to be twenty-four metres long. Too big a job for me, so we have called in a Fence Man. The Fence Man lives not too far away, and M has had him doing work in some of her schools, so we know he does a good job. I contacted him and asked him to come in and assess the job, and he arrived today. I was much relieved when he estimated the length of the fence, and agreed it was exactly twenty-four metres. Maybe I'm getting the hang of this metric nonsense at last.

Luckily, his is one of the trades which is allowed to work during lockdown, because he can do his job without any personal contact. He can communicate with his customers through the window. I imagine that means, when the job is done, that all I have to do is wave a cheque at him through the window. That's even better than contactless payment, and much cheaper. I'm looking forward to getting the job done, it will give me something to watch for a couple of days and will be a nice change from The Sopranos, although when he encounters the berberis I expect the language will be just as colourful.

The DIY and artistic activities continue, in a slightly different direction. I'm refurbishing a toadstool. Yes, you heard me correctly, a toadstool. Not a real one, of course, but one which we've had hanging around in the back garden since time immemorial. It's one of those chainsaw carving ones, made out of a piece of tree trunk, and whatever colour it once was had faded into obscurity, so it was time for a facelift. Now, after a couple of weeks in the shed to dry off and three days of painting, it has a grey stalk and a bright red top with white spots. Tomorrow when the paint is dry, it will get a coat of varnish and then it will be ready to go out on display beside the stone rainbows.

Rainbows and toadstools – what a colourful house we're going to have. No wonder everyone stops and stares when they pass by. Although that may be due to my habit of singing Gaelic songs loudly and tunelessly with the windows open.

Popmaster score: Round 1 – 9 points Round 2 – 12 points

62

Social Distancing Diary – Day 59, a day of activity, indoors and out

Today is Wednesday May 13. A very cold start followed by a very cold day, ending in a very cold evening.

The wooden toadstool is finished, varnished and placed into position at the front of the house to cheer up any passers by. The varnish hasn't dried as clear as I would have liked, so the red colour isn't as bright as it should be. Perhaps I should have read the instructions on the side of the tin: "...do not apply if temperature is below 10°C..." This morning it was down to 2 degrees when I went out for my morning walk and the highest it achieved all day was a balmy 9.3°C. I'm regretting putting away my thermals for the summer.

Also, the fact that the varnish was dated 2013 and has spent seven winters in an unheated shed might have something to do with it. Just goes to prove two of my golden rules: 1. Never throw anything away, and 2. Never, ever, read instructions.

Garden birds are always fascinating and it seems to us that

there are more around this year than ever before. Maybe it's just that we're spending more time at home than usual and we're noticing them more. Today we had a special visitor, a great spotted woodpecker who took a fancy to the nuts in one of our feeders and spent several minutes hanging on and pecking. And he was quite unperturbed by the sparrows who were sharing the feeder with him. Percy, however, hasn't learnt the concept of sharing. And quite honestly neither have I.

We've had woodpeckers in the garden before of course, because they're very common in the woods here, but we've never seen one stay around for so long. Naturally, as soon as M reached for her phone to take a photo, that's when he decided he'd had enough and flew off to perch in Percy's tree. Poor Percy must be feeling rather dull and dowdy alongside such a colourful and glamorous companion.

I also cut the grass today. Strimmed the edges and mowed the laughably named "lawn", avoiding the patches which I re-seeded last week. I've removed the protective fleeces from these areas, the seed hasn't germinated yet but the blackbirds seem to be leaving it alone now. It's obviously lost its attraction for them now that it's a week old. Maybe I should have put a "best before" date on a wee notice beside it, to put them off.

Although it wouldn't work for me. I generally ignore "Best Before" and "Use By" dates. My stomach has a built-in "Feed Me By" date and time, and that overrules any manufacturer's recommendations. Tinned foods, especially, are perfectly edible fifty years (and more) after they've been canned. I'm sure some of the corned beef I've consumed in the past had fought its way across Europe, and took part in the original VE Day celebrations in 1945.

Tomorrow evening is family quiz night, via Zoom. This morning I put the finishing touches to my "movie-star" themed costume. Can't tell you what it is of course, but I shall reveal all tomorrow. And it's my turn to be the quizmaster so I've spent lots of time today making up questions. We have a forty minute session on Zoom, so five rounds of six questions each is enough to fill up the time. On the occasions when I haven't been quizmaster I've consistently come last, so at least this week I'll be spared that indignity.

I hope my contestants are doing their homework because this week the questions are very hard....

Popmaster score: Round 1 – 3 points Round 2 – 18 points

63

～

Social Distancing Diary – Day 60, a day of astrological confusion.

Today is Thursday May 14. Not as cold as yesterday, but still not warm enough for any topless sunbathing, much to everyone's relief.

After a dry walk the rain started, so part of the morning was spent hoovering and dusting. Still very impressed with the new cordless hoover, it's much more obedient than the old dyson, which is currently languishing in the shed waiting for the recycling centre to open. Then it will be heading off to hoover heaven, where no-one ever drops crumbs on the carpet and your bag never needs emptying.

The bin lorry (garbage truck for my American readers) came today. Only for general waste, not for recycling. A week from today I shall get my garden waste bin emptied, for the first time in a couple of months. I've been very good at minimising garden waste, by cutting the grass twice a week without collecting the clippings, but still the bin is full to the top, mostly with moss from my recent scarifying activity. On dry days I leave the bin lid open, and the birds collect scraps of moss to use in their nest building. I wouldn't mind, but they tend to leave trails of moss on the path, which I have to sweep up on a daily basis. Maybe I should have kept the old dyson alive and used it for that task. That would teach it a lesson.

A delivery arrived today, a cardboard box marked "live plants, this way up". This caused a little excitement for M, because she hasn't ordered any plants and our original plant order has been complete for a week or more now. Was it a free gift? An unexpected present from a fan? It was quite heavy, so perhaps a potted plant complete with pot? Opening it carefully so as not to damage the plant within, we were surprised to find – a large plastic tub of birds' peanuts which I had ordered on Sunday from my friend Mr Amazon.

It turns out that the peanut supplier also deals in garden supplies, and so all their boxes are marked as if they contain live plants. End of confusion, and the birds are delighted. Especially Percy, who's far too big to hang onto the nut feeder, but loves trying.

Been keeping track of the (sadly cancelled) exam timetable. This morning it should have been RMPS, which stands for Religious, Moral and Philosophical Studies but is colloquially referred to in Invigilator language as "rumpus". As we all know, a rumpus is a noisy or violent disturbance so it's perhaps not an entirely accurate description, except perhaps when one of my fellow Invigilators gets to the last biscuit before I do.

And in the afternoon it was supposed to be DM, ie Design

and Manufacture. In this exam it is common for the candidate to be given a design task, eg a chair, a letter rack, and they have to describe what materials they would use and how they would construct the item. Fortunately no-one – in my experience, anyway – has so far designed a glass cricket bat. Or a waterproof teabag.

Today's horoscopes are very confusing. In one paper I'm told that Jupiter is remixing my future. So I tried remixing "myfuture" and I got "mute fury". Just about sums up my former relationship with the now-defunct dyson. In another paper, I'm told to "take a moment to collect myself". From where, I ask?

Zoom quiz tonight. I was in the guise of Crocodile Dundee, complete with crocodile. While I adapted the hat myself, and made corks out of scrap wood, I must confess I didn't make the crocodile, it came from Mr Amazon. It's a very scary rubber one which will come in handy for scaring kids away from the door at Halloween time. If we're unlocked by then.

Popmaster score: Round 1 – 18 points Round 2 – 18 points

64

Social Distancing Diary – Day 61, a day of severe pruning, aka indiscriminate hacking

Today is Friday May 15. Warmer today, dry and bright, which meant that the bed sheets had to be changed and the washing machine had to go on. And of course the clean laundry had to be hung on the line. We're lucky to have a proper washing line, not a whirly one, which means that there's room for both of us to hang out the washing at the same time. I start at one end, M at the other, and we meet in the middle. M finished first but we were level pegging right up to the end.

As the day progressed the threat of rain increased, so when M set off on her long afternoon walk I was left in charge of the washing. Which was a big responsibility, because I didn't dare have an afternoon snooze. Luckily I was awake at 3.30 when the rain started, so was able to salvage the washing, which earned me several brownie points. I might even get some beer next time M is shopping.

Fence Man came in his little lorry and dropped off all the materials for the 24-metre fence. He hopes to start work on Monday, if the weather is OK. So I now have several hundred pounds worth of treated wood lying on my (beautiful) lawn. At least that gives me a good excuse not to cut the grass this weekend.

I've warned Fence Man he'll need his gloves on Monday, because of the profusion of birds in this garden, and the resulting effects of their deposits. And we're not talking cash deposits here. And sure enough, the birds have already taken possession of the wood, and have marked it in their own inimitable style. I'm hoping that if they're doing it on the wood, it might mean they leave the cars alone. I'm fed up washing off the results of high-altitude bombing by seagulls and crows.

And in preparation for erecting the fence, the bushes along the edge of the garden had to be cut back. M and I launched into this task immediately after breakfast, armed with an assortment of secateurs and long handled loppers. And thick gloves of course, because the dreaded berberis is one of the offending shrubs. None of these bushes has been trimmed seriously since they were planted, more than twenty years ago, so you can imagine the effort we had to go to, to get them under control. M is ruthless with the loppers, slicing away mercilessly like an enraged Queen Boadicea hacking chunks off some hapless Romans.

Or Corporal Jones and his bayonet: "They don't like it up 'em!"

And I don't bend quite as easily as I used to, which is an inevitable side effect of lockdown eating, so there was some grunting and groaning involved. Also, when I reached the berberis, a few choice expressions, both in English and Gaelic. Their spikes get through the toughest gloves, and my poor fingers are punctured again, after just recovering from last week's ordeal. Sorry dear, I can't possibly wash the dishes. For at least a week.

Interested to read in the financial sections today that the Financial Conduct Authority (no, me neither) has "ordered" car insurance companies to reassess their practice of refusing refunds to drivers who aren't using their cars during the pandemic. Regular readers will remember my attempts to get my car insurer to give me a refund or rebate, and their persistent refusal to do so. They claim to be "the brand you can trust" so let's hope I can trust them to perform a u-turn on their "no refund" stance. If they don't, I shall boycott them completely. Or maybe not. If their next renewal quote saves me enough money to buy some beer, perhaps I shall be a little more forgiving.

Popmaster score: Round 1 – 6 points Round 2 – 3 points

65

⌘

Social Distancing Diary – Day 62, a day of water pipe excitement

Today is Saturday May 16, and because it's the weekend I accompanied M on her morning walk to the riding stables and back. It was threatening rain when we set off, so we wrapped ourselves up in waterproof jackets and trousers. Of course, five minutes later the rain stopped and the sun came out, so we spent the remainder of the walk dry but seriously overheated. Now I know what it feels like to be a prune.

Major excitement in the street today! It started last night, when a Scottish Water van appeared not too far from our house, and from it emerged an engineer-type chap with yellow jacket and hard hat, carrying a selection of drainy/watery/plumbery tools. You can tell from my grasp of the terminology that I know what I'm talking about. I've done the water/drainage course, but I must have been absent the day we covered the naming of parts.

Not long after, we were aware of digging noises further up

the street, frustratingly just out of sight. I even walked along to the end of my drive at bedtime but the action was still just out of sight. We did notice, however, that our bath water was very brown. Which isn't unusual because it's brown every night. After I've been in.

This morning, on the way back from our morning walk, we were intrigued to find four or five Scottish Water vans and trucks, one big lorry and two mechanical diggers, along with several yellow-jacketed workers. And alarmingly, a large volume of water appeared to be exiting one of our neighbours' gardens and was flowing down the street. According to one of those "calming techniques" websites, the sound of flowing water is supposed to be relaxing, but it wasn't working for these guys.

Desperate to know what was going on, but reluctant to stand and stare as the workers tried manfully to control the flood, we adopted the typical British strategy of "walking around the block one more time". And it paid off, because we met up with someone who knew what was going on. It turned out that a major water main had burst underground, in the middle of the neighbour's garden, and a major operation was under way to repair/replace it. This water main dates back to the 1950s, so I suppose it's no great surprise that it has sprung a leak seventy years later. What is surprising is that when the house was built, in the 1980s, no-one noticed a sixteen-inch steel pipe running through the garden. Maybe it was a Friday afternoon for the builders, and the beer was calling. We all know that feeling.

El Gato was absent for 48 hours this week, from Tuesday morning until Thursday morning. We weren't too worried, because he's done this before, but it was still a relief to see he was safe and well when he turned up. Quite often he's been fed by M and has departed by the time I get up in the morning. But even if I don't see him I know that he has been, because he insists on performing his erm, ablutions, in my vegetable garden. Every day. Tonight I plan to sprinkle pepper on the plot to see if that will deter him. If I hear him sneezing tomorrow morning I'll know that I've been successful.

I ran out of space before I could tell you everything that happened yesterday. While we were chopping down our shrubbery I was chatting to my neighbour, who was preparing to cut his grass. His old lawn mower gave up the ghost this year, so he's invested in a new one. And it's a beauty, a shiny orange one. As soon as I saw it I developed a serious case of mower envy. Which is a real thing.

And then last night, M Junior sent us a video clip of Farmer J cutting their grass, with a new ride-on mower. My case of mower envy has now been upgraded from "serious" to "critical".

66

∾

Social Distancing Diary – Day 63, a day of online shopping

Today is Sunday May 17. After a night of rain, it dried up in time for our morning walk. One of the most interesting things about M's walk to the stables is the number of young hares she sees in the fields, playing with each other, and racing up and down the fields at high speed. Haring around, as you might say.

El Gato arrived on the doorstep this morning, looking damp and hungry. Instead of disappearing immediately after eating, he hung around for quite a while, sitting on the doorstep. We worry that passers-by will look at him pitifully and say "oh, that poor cat, why don't they let him in", but he runs away whenever we open the door. Perhaps we should erect a public notice in the garden, with a big arrow pointing towards the doorstep – "this cat does NOT belong to us".

Update on the mail order garden plants – most have survived but some are not very well. In spite of M's attentions and careful nursing some of her bedding plants don't seem to have grown as strong as she had hoped. And my Shirley tomatoes are looking very poorly indeed, out of six plants one has definitely died, four are looking very frail and only one seems to be rallying round. It's said that talking to your plants helps them to thrive, something to do with the oxygen and carbon dioxide you exhale when breathing. Perhaps that's where I went wrong, maybe it wasn't such a good idea breathing "John Smith Bitter" fumes over the poor Shirleys. At least they'll have died happy.

I'm convinced that much of the problems are due to the plants having to travel such a long way to get here, because at that time very few garden suppliers were accepting orders. Now, however, things are much more accessible and our favourite suppliers are accepting orders again. So I spent some time this morning ordering replacement begonias and geraniums for M's containers and hanging baskets. They're coming from a supplier we've used often over the years and so we're sure the quality and packaging will be fine. And the journey will be much shorter, no need for a ferry crossing. And they'll arrive understanding English.

I've also ordered some plants to deter El Gato from visiting my vegetable plot. Last night's experiment with the pepper has had absolutely no effect, perhaps because of all the rain. At bedtime I'd gone out and sprinkled the pepper liberally all around the plot, especially on the potatoes which is his favourite digging area, but this morning there were the usual signs of "buried treasure". In one of today's Sunday papers M spotted an article about this very problem, and the recommendation was to plant something called the "Scaredy Cat Plant", proper name Coleus

Canina. According to the expert in the paper (and no, it wasn't Monty this time, for a change) this plant gives off a smell which is repellent to cats. The most repellent smell I can remember was the Old Spice aftershave we all wore as teenagers back in the 70s. I don't know how it would work with cats but it certainly repelled the girls. Well, that's my excuse anyway.

While I was online, I ordered a replacement kettle for the kitchen. Our kettle, which isn't very old, has lost its ability to switch itself off after it has boiled. So when I do my usual thing of popping the kettle on then going for a shave/walk/spy on the neighbours, I return to find the kitchen full of steam, the kettle handle red hot and the smoke alarm going absolutely mental.

The kettle is coming from my old friend Mr Argos, he's the one who sends me text messages saying: "your delivery is 0 minutes away". He'd better not arrive when I'm in the middle of Popmaster.

This afternoon I broke with tradition and went for a long walk. M set off in one direction and I set off in the other, and we met halfway and walked back together. Thought it would be better for me than my usual Sunday afternoon lounging on the sofa drinking beer. And when I got home guess what I did?

67

⌇

Social Distancing Diary – Day 64, a day of revenge on the cat, and a TV treat

Today is Monday May 18. Another night of heavy rain, but dry enough for a pleasant walk this morning. Because it's a weekday M and I went on our separate routes, hers along to the stables and mine around the woods (about two miles). And it was very peaceful, there was no-one around apart from a couple of joggers. And Angry Dog, who isn't at all angry but unfortunately for him the name seems to have stuck.

I've had loads of feedback about how to keep El Gato and his bodily functions out of my veg patch. Thank you all for your helpful suggestions. I've sorted him out by erecting a barrier. Long ago I had a roll of plastic mesh which I used to make an outdoor run for one of our bunnies and M, whose memory is much better than mine, remembered that it was still lying behind my shed. The mesh, that is, not the bunny.

So with the aid of a couple of rose stakes, some garden canes and cable ties, I've surrounded the veg patch with a mesh fence about three feet high. And at teatime, after El Gato had eaten and had wandered off to perform his ablutions, I watched through the bedroom window and was pleased to see his reaction when he found his favourite toilet area all fenced off. I could almost read his mind: "Aargh, another public toilet closed. These council cutbacks are getting worse".

This arrangement is only temporary, of course. After two or three weeks I'm hoping he'll have found another favoured spot to carry out his duties, and by then the scaredy-cat plants will have arrived and been planted, so the fence can come down and the mesh returned to its resting place behind the shed. Just goes to reinforce the wisdom of my policy of never throwing anything away. Although I need M to help me remember where I've put it.

Fence Man arrived this morning, as planned. He didn't take long to rip down the old fence, the posts were so rotten they almost fell down by themselves. Then the hard part for him was digging holes for the new posts, the ground is full of tree roots and boulders. I noticed he has an electronic device which he scans over the ground before he digs the holes, to alert him to any electric cables or water pipes buried there. It's a pity that the builders didn't do the same forty years ago when they built that house across the street. They might have noticed a blooming great water main under the garden.

Scottish Water were working there all day Saturday, most of yesterday, and they're back again today. The poor owner's garden is completely destroyed, I hope he'll be suitably compensated because none of this is his fault. Usually we're bombarded by cold callers on the phone, offering to help us claim compensation for accidents, injuries etc, but there haven't been any such calls since lockdown began. I think this is because government restrictions have been imposed to stop these organisations trying to cash in on the coronavirus crisis. I think I'll start calling them up and taunting them with tales of fictitious accidents. And I'll try to time my calls for when they're just about to sit down to dinner, see how they like it.

This afternoon I joined M for the long walk, which I had always estimated as being six miles. But today, due partly to a following wind, we completed it in an hour and forty-five minutes rather than the normal two hours, so I'm guessing my original figure was an overestimate and the true distance is probably nearer five miles. But it's still a major trek for a pensioner with a pole and a sore ankle.

And there was a very good reason for this increased exercise, which I shall reveal to you tomorrow.

Finally, on tonight's Chelsea Flower Show programme on BBC, a treat for M and for me. The Blessed Monty interviewing the Fragrant Joanna. Both of them on screen at the same time. Heaven.

Popmaster score: Round 1 – 3 points Round 2 – 15 points

68

Social Distancing Diary – Day 65, a day of a healthy lifestyle change

Today is Tuesday May 19, drizzly in the morning but dry and warm for the rest of the day. Fence man is back, working hard, and should be finished tomorrow. Meantime there's a gap where my gate used to be, and that's where El Gato appears from, strolling in casually. He probably thinks we've removed the gate just for him.

Lovely Italian neighbour has given me four frozen pizzas. She makes her own pizzas, in traditional Italian style, and I've never tasted better ones anywhere. And that includes Rome and Florence. I've been to Florence twice, once with M and once on my own to attend a Moto GP race. In the market square there's a bronze statue of a wild boar, and tradition has it that if you rub his nose (and give him a coin of course) you'll return to Florence. His is known as "Il Porcellino", which is Italian for "piglet", although he's obviously a fully-grown and handsome example of piggy masculinity. And while the rest of him is a dull bronze colour, his snout is shiny and wearing away with all the tourists rubbing it. No wonder he's wild.

Anyway, I've rubbed his nose on both of my visits, so the legend predicts that I will return. Certainly won't be this year though, even Il Porcellino is in social isolation right now. I hope he's wearing a mask.

I've been busy and creative again, for this week's zoom quiz, who's theme is a character from the world of drama. This week's effort is in two parts, one supplied by Mr Amazon and one made by me, using my old favourite resource, the empty cereal packet. Crunchy Nut cornflakes, if you must know. So I've been busy in the shed with the scissors and there's glue and paint flying everywhere.

And now, here's the reason for extra exercise that I told you about yesterday. I've decided to adopt a new healthy lifestyle. Yes, really. I've been horrified by the way my weight has ballooned since lockdown started. Sadly my waistline has ballooned too, and no matter how I try, sometimes I accidentally catch sight of myself in the bathroom mirror. No wonder I have nightmares.

According to the NHS website I need to lose around 10lbs to achieve my normal healthy weight , so something needs to be done. And here's the plan. No more snacks between meals, absolutely no chocolate, no beer except at weekends, and extra walking. To reinforce this regime and stay motivated I'm going to weigh myself every Friday and post the results on a chart on the fridge door. I may need a bigger piece of paper.

I'm embarrassed to share the actual figures with you, but by sharing the plan with you, I hope that my resolve will be bolstered and that I won't have a relapse. Because if I do, I know how supportive you are, and I also know that you won't hesitate to slag me off when my willpower crumbles. That's the same willpower that I used to give up smoking in 1983. And 1984. And again in 1987.

However, there was some news yesterday which will give my resolve a very hard test. Harry Gow, of dream ring fame, is opening his Dingwall shop. Today. Twenty-four hours after I've imposed a strict "no snacks" diet on myself. I suspect that next time M goes to Dingwall she'll very likely come home with a dream ring, so the question will be: can I force myself to save it and have it for my pudding at teatime, or will I crumble and scoff it immediately? What a test of strength! I'll need to upgrade my willpower from "wet rice pudding" to "wall of steel".

And again, for the second day in a row, I walked the marathon five-mile route with M in the afternoon. And I do two miles every morning on my own anyway, so that's about seven miles a day I'm doing. I'm hoping that I'll be rewarded with a significant weight loss by Friday. Depending on the dream ring intake.

Popmaster score: Round 1 – 9 points Round 2 – 15 points

69

∾

Social Distancing Diary – Day 66, a day of longing for London Town

Today is Wednesday May 20, and I shouldn't be here. According to my pocket diary M and I should be in London tonight, living the dream in a nice hotel in Chelsea before visiting the famous flower show tomorrow. We were due to fly with easyJet from Inverness to Gatwick, then the Gatwick Express train into central London. I even have two Oyster Cards ready topped up for us to travel by bus or tube within the city. However, I understand that Oyster Cards never go out of date so the credit will be useful at some point in the future. And unlike real oysters, apparently you can use them even when there isn't an "R" in the month. Although I believe they can make you ill if you eat them. Maybe they should carry a health warning.

The vegetable plot is developing nicely. Early and second early potatoes are through the ground and doing well, I have to watch out for frosty nights and cover them with bubble wrap. So far, no frost damage has occurred. The maincrop ones are (sensibly) staying underground and sadly, the carrots seem to be doing the same. I sowed them direct into the ground on Day 44, so they've had twenty-two days in which to germinate. According to the packet, they should appear ten to twelve days after sowing so either they're particularly lazy or some underground beastie has eaten them. Or maybe I've sowed them too deep and they're coming through in Wogga Wogga.

Fence Man has finished the job, and a very good job it is too. We now have a robust fence high enough to keep unwanted visitors out, and to keep Dog F in when she visits. And we have a gate, so El Gato won't be able to simply wander in at mealtimes, if he wants to eat he'll have to work on his high jump skills.

As soon as Fence Man was finished, I cut the grass where his materials had been stored. In doing so I was very happy to note that the one (possibly two) year old grass seed I sowed away back on Day 54 has germinated. Lots of fresh little green shoots have appeared, so my ploy of covering the area with a fleece to keep the birds off has worked. I still have some of that seed left over so I may try reseeding another patch, if I can summon up enough energy to do the moss raking first. Which I couldn't do today because it was far too hot for physical work. And I was far too weak with hunger.

In fact it was so warm, I thought it would have been a perfect afternoon for sitting in the garden drinking an ice cold beer. Sadly, I'm on day 3 of the self-imposed diet so no beer allowed until Friday. Who's idea was this anyway? Oh, it was mine.

But to be honest, the diet is going well. Not a snack has passed my lips between meals, no chocolate or alcohol, and plenty extra exercise. I'm feeling very self-righteous but not seeing any waistline improvement yet. I'm resisting weighing myself until Friday, when I hope to see a reduction. I've given myself the target of losing the necessary 10lbs by the time M Junior's baby arrives, which is less than seven weeks, so that's my incentive. And if I don't quite achieve it I can always shed at least a pound by getting M to cut my hair.

So instead of lounging with beer, I once again accompanied M on the five mile circuit and for the first time this year I went without a jacket. This was a very daring act because we have an old saying here in Scotland: "Ne'er cast a cloot till May is oot". Overseas readers may need to google that one.

So instead of a posh hotel in London with a glamorous receptionist and an attentive wine waiter, it's goodnight from a modest bungalow in Ross-shire with a persistent crow and a demanding cat.

Popmaster score: Round 1 – 9 points Round 2 – 3 points

70

∽

Social Distancing Diary – Day 67, a day of housework and paintwork

Today is Thursday 21 May, cooler than yesterday but very comfortable for my morning walk. As I told you yesterday, we should have wakened up in a smart London hotel today, but no such luck. No pampering, no buffet breakfast, no complimentary newspaper. I even had to make my own bed.

Today was a big day for the garden refuse bin, it got emptied for the first time since before lockdown. Boy, was I glad to get it emptied. It was full to the brim with all my moss rakings from a couple of weeks ago, and some very hostile berberis branches lurking near the top to catch any unwary bin man who might innocently stick his hand in there to clear a blockage.

No lawn clippings though, because my policy of twice-weekly mowing and leaving the clippings uncollected seems to be paying off. My lawn has never looked so good, even though it's at least seventy-five percent moss.

Today I did hoovering and dusting. M and I have come to an

arrangement whereby I'm excused cleaning the bathroom and kitchen surfaces because of my sore hands. Yes, I'm still using the berberis pruning injuries as an excuse a full week later. But I haven't been able to come up with a plausible excuse to avoid hoovering and dusting, so I have to do that while she scrubs the bath, the sink and other, less savoury, fittings. I think I probably got the best deal because the shark is a pleasure to use – no cables to get my feet tangled up with, no problems getting it to follow me round corners, and because it has a kind of double-jointy thing in the middle I can reach under the furniture without having to bend. Which is a bonus for anyone with a midriff bulge like mine.

Remember the wooden toadstool I renovated and painted a week or two ago? Well, it's back in the shed for some intensive care. I was horrified to notice the other day that the recent rain had washed off some of the white paint, and left it looking very shabby. Of course, once again it wasn't my fault, it was the inferior paint to blame. That's my claim, anyway. The white spots on the toadstool were done with simple poster paint, but I thought that a coat of varnish would keep it safe from rain. Unfortunately the varnish is at least as old as Noah's beard, and appears to have the same degree of water resistance.

A trip to B&Q for paint would involve a drive to Inverness, and I can't in all conscience class that as an essential journey, even if I was allowed to leave home, so I have had a thorough search of my shed for some decent paint. And I've found some proper wood preservative paint at the back of a shelf. It's not white but it's close enough, and after a stir and a test on some scrap wood I think it will be all right. It says on the tin that it's rainproof within an hour and this time I hope it lasts longer than an hour.

Speaking of paint, the paintwork on my car is constantly being targeted by incontinent high flying birds, so I had to wash it again today. The funny thing is that they don't seem to go for M's car, only mine. So as an experiment, and because it's good for the cars anyway, we've moved my one to the rear of the drive and M's one to the front, and she'll use it for shopping. But strangely enough it hasn't made any difference to the birds. This morning I was sad to see that they've once more ignored M's car and splattered mine with their droppings, from a great height apparently. I can't explain it, perhaps "FIAT" stands for "Fouling Is Absolutely Terrible" in bird language, and "MAZDA" means "Mandatory Attack Zone, Defecate Abundantly".

Zoom quiz tonight. My drama character was Hamlet, the Prince of Denmark, with a home-made cardboard crown and a plastic skull from Mr Amazon. As usual, I came last. Alas! Poor Yorick.

Popmaster score: Round 1 – 9 points Round 2 – 12 points

71

～

Social Distancing Diary – Day 68, a day of weight loss. And a dream ring.

Today is Friday May 22. Heavy rain during the night and still raining when M set off on her morning walk. Wisely, I remained in bed for an extra half hour before going on my walk, and by then the rain had stopped. We each took an umbrella, M's was soaked but I never needed to open mine. Just goes to show that sometimes the early bird catches the worm, and the pneumonia, but the later one stays dry and smug.

Delighted to report that I have lost five pounds in weight since last week. I know that it's typical to lose a significant amount in the first week, then the rate of loss slows down, but I'm still feeling proud of myself. Only another seven to go, in six weeks, to reach my target. The bathroom scales were very surprised when I stepped on this morning. If they could speak they would have said: "who's this?"

Farmer J is in the papers today, he's fronting a #keeptalking campaign, which is aimed at farmers who feel isolated and would like to chat to someone. I hope none of them phone me for a chat because I know nothing about farming. Until I met Farmer J, I thought bacon grew on trees and milk came from coconuts. And I was horrified when he told me which part of the chicken's anatomy the eggs come out of.

M went on her weekly shopping trip to Dingwall and, as usual, managed to get almost everything on her list. And, as a bonus, she brought me a DREAM RING from Harry Gow's newly reopened shop! It's the first one I've had for several weeks and I was really excited. (And she paid full price for it – wouldn't you think old Harry would let me have a freebie, after all the free advertising I give him?) Anyway, how was I to reconcile this calorie-laden treat with my new diet regime? Well, using willpower so strong I even amazed myself, I cut it in half, and had half with my lunch and the other half as part of my dinner. And after lunch, of course, I walked the five-mile circuit with M, thereby cancelling out the dream ring calories.

There's a chart in one of the papers today which equates certain activities with the number of calories burnt. For example, washing the car burns off 234 calories an hour, so the dive-bombing birds who keep targeting my car are actually assisting with my weight loss. Gardening for an hour equates to 162 calories, so my twice-weekly grass cutting is also contributing. Indeed it's surprising that I'm not wasting away altogether.

But the best news is that walking burns off 300 calories an hour, so my afternoon walk has earned me the right to drink three pints of beer. Or two pints of beer and a dream ring, so I allowed myself one bottle of beer with my dinner, for the first time this week.

One thing that M failed to get while shopping is a nut feeder for the birds. We have a couple of feeders hanging on the bird table, one full of seeds and the other with peanuts. It's great fun watching the sparrows and blue tits hanging on the feeders, pecking through the mesh, but it's not such fun seeing Percy and his pals trying to do the same. These crows are so big and clumsy, they invariably knock the nut feeder on to the ground, and after a few of these incidents it comes apart and has to be mended. By me, in the intensive care department of the shed along with rain-damaged toadstools and any other casualties.

Last night, in frustration after having repaired it several times in the past few weeks, I assembled it with a liberal dash of super-glue in the hope that it would now be unbreakable. And for a change, I didn't glue anything to my own hand. OK Percy, come and give it a try if you think you're hard enough.

Popmaster score: Round 1 – 9 points Round 2 – 3 points

72

Social Distancing Diary – Day 69, a day of wind. And a Latin lesson.

Today is Saturday May 23, and a blowy blustery day it is. On our morning walk to the stables we were impressed to note that the potholes in the road have been filled in. Which is long overdue, because some of them were very deep. I hope the road menders didn't harm any of the fish that were living in them.

Immediately after breakfast M sprang into action, changing and washing the bedding. For my part, I helped hang out the washing, which was very difficult in the blustery conditions. Especially when my underwear billowed in the wind like a sail, and threatened to waft me away, now that I'm as light as a feather after a whole week of no snacking.

The rain-damaged toadstool has now been refurbished, with two coats of red paint topped off with two coats of white painted spots. I'll keep it in the shed for a couple of days just to make sure the paint is fully hardened before I put it out in front of the house again. No varnish this time because the paint is waterproof, according to the tin. I'm not sure how old the paint is exactly, but the instructions on the tin are in Latin. Did you know that "stir well" in Latin is "etiam suscitare"? Thank goodness for Google Translate, or I might have applied the paint without stirring.

Anyway, I'm sure Etiam Suscitare was one of those ultra-violent gangsters from The Sopranos. Wasn't he the one who ended up at the bottom of the Hudson river, wrapped up in black polythene and wearing concrete overshoes?

I hope no-one from the Mafia is reading this diary. I'd hate to be woken up in the middle of the night by gun toting hoodlums, and taken away in the boot of a car before being "whacked" and dumped over the side of the Stornoway ferry. Imagine being trawled up from the sea bed by a couple of prawn fishermen from Skye – "Aye, aye Lachie, what's this?" "Och Callum, that's the third one this week. Looks like the work of those lads in the Plockton Mafia, they've become extra violent since they heard the Mod was cancelled".

M went to Dingwall today, to get her electric meter top-up. Rather disappointingly she didn't bring me back a dream ring. Apparently a dream ring every day is incompatible with my dietary regime, so it's likely to be a once-a-week treat. She did bring me back The Times, though, in the hope that the crossword will keep me out of her hair for a few hours. Or days. Recently I've had immense difficulty finishing the Times crossword, for at least the last two weeks I've not managed it without the help of Mr Google. Either my brain is getting weaker or the clues are getting more obscure. Just look at today's 1 across: "When horse is gone, cut round top field (6)". What do I know about horses or fields? Nothing. Perhaps Farmer J can help. [*afternote: don't write in, I solved it already*]

And, apart from shopping, M is a very happy bunny today. A couple of weeks ago she ordered a delivery of compost for her plants, and it has arrived. Two forty-litre bags and a twenty-litre one which, in my non-metric language is two half-hundred-weights and a twenty-eight pounder. So, immediately after her Dingwall trip she retired to her potting shed and transplanted all her successful seedlings into bigger pots and containers. Meanwhile, my poor Shirley tomatoes are still struggling to survive so it's obvious which of us has the greenest fingers.

On the plus side, my two original tomato plants are doing really well, with loads of flower trusses which (hopefully) will yield loads of tasty toms in the summer. Tasty Tom? Now there's another good name for a Sopranos character. Unless he gets shoved into the incinerator by Tony and his thuggish pals, then I suppose he'll be Toasty Tom.

73

◈

Social Distancing Diary – Day 70, a day of fresh air and carrots

Today is Sunday May 24, and after a stormy night a much quieter day dawned. Still slightly damp, but M and I managed our morning walk to the stables and back without getting rained on. And on the afternoon walk we just had some light showers, so no fear of catching pneumonia today.

Lots of wildlife out today, a variety of small birds, plus squads of pheasants in the fields of young barley. And in another field a couple of hares and a young roe deer who showed no fear as we approached. Also, for the first time in a few years we heard a cuckoo. That's the bird whose claim to fame is laying eggs in other bird's nests, then abandoning them. Kind of like a feathered version of Rod Stewart or Mick Jagger, without the inconvenience of having to pay child maintenance.

I'm sure nature wasn't so prolific before lockdown, or maybe it's just that we're more observant nowadays because we're walking more and driving less. And with fewer pollutants in the atmosphere maybe the birdies and beasties are thriving in the fresh air. Walking in the fresh air is good for people too. According to the NHS website the benefits include enhanced mood and stimulated appetite. So here I am on the diet from hell, feeling happier but hungrier.

Sunday in our house is traditionally a day when nothing happens. Morning walk, breakfast, then settle down with the Sunday papers. I read Scotland on Sunday from cover to cover, except for the sports pages, and it takes anything from one to two hours, depending on how quickly I fall asleep in the armchair. I usually make it as far as the middle pages, which is the fashion section, and that's enough to send me off. Today's featured fashion was jumpsuits but the models were posing sedately and didn't appear to be doing very much jumping.

El Gato turned up this morning, for the first time since Friday. There's a photo in one of the papers this weekend of a Scottish Wildcat, which is an endangered species. There's still a few in the wild, up here in the north of Scotland, but breeding with domestic cats is diluting the species and making them rarer and rarer. Pity it doesn't work that way with people, I can think of a few wild ones who would benefit from some diluting. Hesitate to name names, but there's a Kim in there. And a Vlad, a Donald and a Boris.

Anyway, I'm sure El Gato is part wildcat, he has the same colouring and distinctive ringed tail as the one in the paper. I'm trying to get a photo of him for you to compare with the real wildcat, but he's very shy and runs away as soon as he sees the camera. I think he may have been a member of the Royal family in a previous life.

I have very mixed success with phone photos, often ending up with a selfie by mistake, and sometimes I hit the wrong setting altogether and get a video instead of a photo. And sometimes it's a video selfie, which is the ultimate embarrassment.

Good news on the garden front – at last the carrots have appeared! After a spell of wet but warm conditions they've finally popped their heads above the ground. The odd thing is that they haven't appeared where I was expecting them to. When I sowed the seeds I strung a piece of twine along the row to remind me where they were, but the seedlings have come through an inch to the left of the line. Either the wee carrots have taken an underground diversion, or someone has sneaked in and moved the string.

Or maybe there was an earthquake during the night which I missed. I did hear some very loud rumbling but I assumed it was just my stomach. On a good day it can register ten on the Richter Scale. Or is it the Rifter Scale?

74

〰

Social Distancing Diary – Day 71, a day of high pressure

Today is Monday May 25, and as the end of the month peeps over the horizon, there's some hope at last of lockdown being gently eased. If all goes well, on Thursday we'll be able to have (outdoor) meetings with other households, sit in public places and resume some outdoor activities, eg golf and angling. I've never played golf, and it's many years since I went fishing. I thought I might raid the attic, because there's still a fly fishing rod lurking up there, but on reflection I decided it would be a waste of time. I don't have a lot of luck with hooks. In the past I've impaled a finger and an ear, and on one memorable occasion I caught the back of my own head whilst casting, and launched my hat into the river. I never saw that hat again.

I have an image in my head of a class of wee squids sitting in a semi circle at the bottom of the sea, listening to a story told by a wise old octopus wearing a baseball cap bearing the legend:

"I ♡ Dingwall".

There's also a plan for local authority recycling centres to open, but with certain restrictions. In our council area the restrictions are that they will only accept bagged household waste, and garden waste. Which is no use to me because my wee plastic shed is full of scrap metal and electrical items. There's a dud table lamp in there, along with last week's blown-up kettle and, of course, the dreaded, and now deceased, Dyson. I will be so happy to see it landing in the skip. Also in there is the metal rail from the old kitchen blind, a broken bike rack for the car and an unidentified rusty old metal rod with a flat bit on the end. We don't know where it came from, we don't know what it's for, and we don't know how to get rid of it. Rather like the cat.

Today was a busy one, and a high pressure one. Although I knew that today was BBC Radio 2's All Day Popmaster, I simply didn't have time to take part, with the exception of my usual 10.30 version. And I knew I'd be having a Zoom meeting at 11.00 so I had a very narrow window between breakfast and 10.30 to get lots done. And, in spite of my strict diet, I'm still the wrong shape for narrow windows.

Immediately after breakfast I headed out to the garden to try to get some vegetable planting done. The plot is filling up nicely. I've put in three rows each of broccoli and brussels sprouts, one row of one variety of beetroot and two rows of another variety. All these little plants have been grown from seed by M in her greenhouse, and have been used to getting pampered by her. But now they're out in the big bad world and they'll have to learn to survive, just like children leaving home. Except we don't have to pay their phone bill, or buy them a car.

You'll have noticed that everything I planted today begins

with B. And next door to them are the carrots, so that's C accounted for. But I don't have anything beginning with A. Asparagus takes too long to grow, artichokes are too posh for me, maybe I'll try an avocado. They're sweet on the outside but very hard at heart. Very popular with bank managers or car insurance agents, I should imagine.

Then I popped my muddy gardening clothes in the wash and set the machine going before Popmaster. Immediately after Round Two I only had ten minutes left before Zoom time, so I didn't even have time to listen to the "3 in 10" round. Got the washing hung out, made a cup of tea, got the laptop switched on and logged into Zoom, just in time. Phew.

Then it was lunchtime, then it was time for the long walk, then I had an hour to myself for the first time today, and a chance to catch up with the papers. Bored in lockdown? I simply don't have the time.

Popmaster score: Round 1 – 6 points Round 2 – 9 points

75

~

Social Distancing Diary – Day 72, a day of school memories. Painful ones.

Today is Tuesday May 26. Cut the grass today, and had to use the box to collect the clippings because it hadn't been cut since last Wednesday. My twice-weekly cut fell by the wayside because of the wild and wet weather at the weekend. Also because of the windy conditions there were lots of stray leaves to be gathered up. Living as we do on the edge of a woodland area, and because most of our neighbours have trees in their gardens, we're always inundated with leaves. Plenty beech leaves, birch leaves and even oak leaves, but no fig leaves. Which is probably just as well, because there might otherwise be a temptation to try one as a fashion accessory.

When we moved into this house more than twenty years ago there were several mature trees, limes and birch, and because they were blocking our light and threatening out foundations we had them all chopped down. We left the trunk of one of the limes standing, and that's where one end of our washing line is secured to. It's also a favourite perching spot for Percy. From where he can survey the whole garden and see where the bread-crumbs are. And he can quickly spot the kitchen door opening, which is his cue to make a sharp exit.

Luckily the garden refuse bin got emptied on Thursday so I have plenty of space for all this green waste. I do have a compost bin, but it's full, and has been for a couple of years, with the result that the compost inside it is well rotted and in good condition. In fact I dug some of it in to the veg plot this year, so I hope there's no diseases in it. I'd hate to be responsible for the demise of M's carefully cultivated beetroots.

I ran out of space yesterday to tell you about the Zoom meeting I had with some old friends and former colleagues. We're all involved in education in some capacity or another, and inevitably the conversation came round to the Scottish Government's plan to reopen schools on August 11. The biggest issue is going to be maintaining social distancing between pupils, so desks will have to be two metres apart. This means that pupil numbers will inevitably be smaller, so that maybe only half a class can be in school at one time. This will stop kids whispering to each other when teacher isn't looking, and will also eliminate the age-old practice of copying answers from your brainier neighbour.

And if your neighbour is smellier, rather than brainier, then you will have a nice exclusion zone of fresh air between your sensitive nose and his personal hygiene issues.

Another age-old practice which will be wiped out is the passing of romantic notes from a teenage romeo to the object of his testosterone-laden affections. Many a teenage girl's first experience of courtship was the receipt of a grubby little note which had been written several days before and had been kept in a warm germ-laden pocket while the courage was plucked up to hand it over.

Of course, the teachers will have to maintain the two-metre distance from the pupils too, which would have been impossible when I was in school. In my day teachers had to be within striking distance, to correct any misdemeanours swiftly and efficiently. Favoured methods were a simple slap on the back of the head, the ruler across the knuckles and, of course, the dreaded tawse. For my overseas readers, the tawse was a particularly savage leather belt applied to the palm of the hand with varying degrees of force and accuracy. Sometimes, with weaker teachers, it was little more than a light tap, but some of the stronger teachers wielded it with some skill and very painful results.

I'm surprised that most of us grew up into civilised, non-violent citizens. Some of the girls did, too.

Popmaster score: Round 1 – 9 points Round 2 – 15 points

76

Social Distancing Diary – Day 73, a day of counting steps

Today is Wednesday May 27. A very pleasant start, nice and cool for my morning walk, but became much warmer as the day went on. And on my morning walk I met Angry Dog, whom I hadn't seen since Friday. I was worried that he'd changed his route, or his timetable, to avoid me but as soon as he saw me he abandoned his owner and ran to me for his treat. Obviously greed is stronger than loyalty. Works for me too.

Also ever present this week is El Gato, who has been coming morning and evening as usual, but has now added mid-mornings to his visiting schedule. And after he has been fed, instead of wandering off as before, he now remains sitting on the doorstep as if he owns the place. Just as an experiment, I left the kitchen door open and sat quietly, to see if he was brave enough to come into the house. The next thing I saw was his cheeky wee face peeking round the kitchen unit as he ventured inside to check for food. As soon as I stood up he fled, of course, but he's definitely getting braver. I often venture into the kitchen looking for food too, but I get chased more violently than the cat does.

In response to a question from a friend about how many steps I'm doing under my new diet and exercise regime, I've resurrected my fitbit from a few years ago. I wore it constantly for two years, to ensure I was doing ten thousand steps a day, but I abandoned it in 2017 and just got out of the habit. Anyway, I found it and charged it up on Monday and have worn it ever since. The figures are surprising. By bedtime last night I had covered almost twenty thousand steps, and a distance of 8.4 miles. And today I did twenty-two thousand steps and 9.3 miles. And all without a single snack. Phew no wonder I'm weak.

But the surprising thing is that once I worked out the distances, I established that my morning walk is two miles, my afternoon one just over five miles, and so where do the remaining miles come from? Do I really cover such long distances just pottering around the house and garden? I do make frequent trips to the kitchen to gaze longingly at the forbidden fridge, so maybe that accounts for it.

Also on the diet and exercise front, I'm happy to report that my dodgy ankle seems to be much improved. Can't explain why, but perhaps the loss of those few pounds in weight has contributed. Initially when I set off there's a little pain, but after half a mile or so it goes away and then I feel that I could walk for ever. I'm still using my Pensioner's Pole though. I'm not sure I really need it for support but it's handy for fending off over-enthusiastic small children who dare to venture inside my two-metre exclusion zone.

M has been busy this week, setting up classrooms in her schools to test how the two-metre distancing will work when pupils go back. She photographs the classrooms once she's set them up and sends the pics to the head teacher, because of course no-one apart from M is allowed to enter the school building yet. In some of the older schools the rooms are varied in size, some can accommodate a dozen kids, but others only three or four. So the pupils will be able to attend only part-time, perhaps a week at a time, with the rest of their learning being at home in what the Scottish Government is calling "blended learning". Perhaps the age-old excuse: "the dog ate my homework" will have to be updated: "please miss, my homework fell in the blender".

There's a plan to use village halls, leisure centres and any other available spaces as additional classrooms, to allow the maximum number of pupils to attend. And to staff these extra facilities, there is to be an initiative to bring retired teachers back into employment. Kids, you better hope they don't bring back any of mine.

Popmaster score: Round 1 – 9 points Round 2 – 9 points

77

⌇⌇

Social Distancing Diary – Day 74, a day of veggie-jokes

Today is Thursday May 28. A damp start after quite a bit of overnight rain, not so good for walking but very good indeed for the veg garden. One of the varieties of beetroot I planted the other day was looking quite limp and I was beginning to worry that I'd killed them. M assured me that they'd be all right but wouldn't allow me to water them, saying artificial watering doesn't do as much good as natural rainfall. And guess what? She was right. By this morning they had perked up considerably. Just like I do on the rare occasions when I get a drink.

And I was perked up this morning too, because along with the rain there was a drop in temperature and it was much more comfortable. These past couple of days have been uncomfortably warm for me, especially when cutting grass or pottering in the garden. I'm not a sun worshipper, and much prefer to be cool. Perhaps I was an Arctic explorer in a previous life. Or a polar bear.

Today was bin day which is always a highlight of the week.

How sad is that? However it helps me remember what day it is, and that the weekend is only two days away. Had a chat with Bin Lorry Man, who was also relieved that it was a little cooler today. Poor chaps have to wear all sorts of protective gear and it must be like working in a Turkish bath sometimes. Not that I would know anything about Turkish baths. M has enough trouble getting me to take a normal bath.

And just to make the day a domestic success, I did the hoovering and dusting in the morning, and at lunchtime when the sun came out I got a washing out to dry. I really don't know how I manage to cope with all this excitement.

Tonight I should have been attending a Gaelic Choirs concert in Inverness Cathedral. There were a few choirs due to take part, senior and junior ones, and in the splendid setting of the cathedral it would have been a very special evening. Cancelled because of covid-19, of course, like everything else I was planning this year. It was to be one of a series of events leading up to Saturday, which was the planned date for the 2020 Gathering, a one-day outdoor festival of traditional Scottish music. I'm sorry to miss it, I had a ticket and everything so I didn't even need to sneak in under the fence.

But there's a little light on the horizon. Nicola has announced an easing of some of our lockdown restrictions. From tomorrow we're allowed to meet people from other households, outdoors in parks and private gardens, with distancing of course. Outdoor sports, such as golf, tennis and bowls will be permitted, while recycling facilities and drive-through restaurants will reopen.

And we're allowed to sunbathe in the park but I think I'll give that a miss. The good people of Dingwall have suffered enough trauma without having to witness me lying in the park like a particularly pale beached whale.

Tonight was our weekly Zoom quiz with M and friends. This week's theme wasn't a dressing up one, it was a challenge to produce a vegetable (vegepal!) and tell a joke about it. And it had to be an original joke, not one stolen from the internet! M provided me with a yellow pepper, and I stuck two eyes on to it. And it took me the entire week to come up with a joke: "what pepper is most in demand during lockdown? - Toilet pepper!" And just to reinforce the joke I revealed a half-used toilet roll and placed the pepper on top of it. Funny? Let's just say none of them rolled on the floor, or burst any blood vessels.

BUT – for the first time, Team Thomson won the quiz! By a considerable margin. And at 8pm all the neighbours came out and clapped for us, so that was nice.

Popmaster score: Round 1 – 12 points Round 2 – 6 points

78

Social Distancing Diary – Day 75, a day of assembly. And disassembly. And reassembly.

Today is Friday May 29, and the forecasters told us it was to be the hottest day of the year so far. And they were right. By mid-day our weather station was showing 24C. But first thing in the morning it was cool and misty, so for a change I had my long walk before breakfast, while it was still comfortable. Bad news for Angry Dog, because I wasn't on his route today, so he missed out on a treat. Although I did share a treat with the wee dog next door, who sees me as a soft touch and always comes to the fence whenever I'm out in the garden.

Friday morning is weigh-in time. Today the scales told me I had lost a further pound since last week, so that leaves six lbs still to lose if I'm to reach my target before I become a grandad. I'm still snack-free, and alcohol-free except at weekends, and I'm exercising more than ever. If I can keep on losing a pound a week the sacrifice will be worthwhile. No dream ring today, but had one small low alcohol beer at teatime to celebrate.

One of my annual traditions took place today. Every year, around the last weekend of May, the ceremony of Putting Up The Gazebo gets under way. Along with rising temperatures and longer daylight, this is one of the signs that summer is actually here. And it has to be carried out with the correct actions and in the correct order, like all traditional events, such as the World Bog Snorkelling Championships or the Yorkshire Pudding Boat Race. And no, I haven't made these up.

First then, comes the locating of the actual gazebo. In an ideal world it has been carefully packed and put away the previous autumn, with all the parts clearly labelled. However we don't live in an ideal world, so some rummaging has to take place, in both the big wooden shed and the wee plastic one. Next comes the sorting out of the poles. These come in various sizes and fit together in a certain way in order to create the frame. There follows a spell of trial and error while it is established which are the roof, which are the legs, and why are there four left over?

Then, once the frame has been assembled, disassembled and reassembled a few times, comes the really tricky part – the fitting of the canopy. It's not tricky because of difficulty, it's tricky because of the dimensions. At its apex the gazebo is a massive nine feet high, and even on my tippy-toes I can't get anywhere near to that, so a massive operation gets under way, involving a shaky stepladder, a long reach garden rake and a lot (and I mean a lot) of grunting. At last everything is in place, pegged down and ready for relaxing in for the rest of the summer. Or until the first gale comes along and blows it away. And it lands on the Ullapool road, like some sort of mad green canvas UFO. That would give them something to talk about on the Stornoway ferry.

Today marked another annual event - "wear yellow for the Highland Hospice" day. So I dug out my only yellow-ish garment, an ancient but honourable mustard coloured polo shirt. I don't think I've worn it since last year's "wear yellow" day so at that rate of usage, I'm hopeful it won't wear out too soon.

I forgot to tell you yesterday that I completed the Times Wednesday crossword in record time this week – less than 24 hours. And I only had to resort to the Chambers Dictionary once, to discover a new word, "saraband". I'm not going to tell you what it means, you'll have to look it up yourself. But one thing is certain, it wasn't in common use in the more remote parts of the Scottish Highlands when I was a boy.

Popmaster score: Round 1 – 3 points Round 2 – 12 points

79

~~

Social Distancing Diary – Day 76, a day of grooming

Today is Saturday May 30. M doesn't work weekends so we had the long walk together before breakfast, while the day was still cool. And it was very quiet, not many people around at that time in the morning, just one or two horse owners visiting their animals, going into the stable with a brush and shovel, and coming out with a steaming barrow load of whatever the horse has produced during the night. And it seems some horses have quite busy nights.

The polite term for what's in the barrow is "organic fertiliser", but apparently the Queen refers to it as "arisings". Annus horribilis indeed.

For the first time in around 85 days, I've had my hair cut! No, not by a professional hairdresser, stylist or even barber, but by M, on a wooden stool outside the shed. I've always kept my hair short, apart from a few years in the late 60s / early 70s, when glam rock was at its height and I sported long curly locks and

Noddy Holder sideburns. Overseas readers and those under 60 might need to Google "Noddy Holder".

And especially since I started going thin on top, I've become even more keen on keeping it short. I always think nothing looks worse than a balding head with long straggly hair hanging down at the sides. With the possible exception of a comb-over, held in place by liberal sprays of starch. That's the style that looks immaculate, until you have to come down the stairs of an aircraft in the wind. Particularly when exiting Air Force One.

So for years now I've been a barber's dream client. No fancy styles, no special shapes, no patterns cut into the back of my neck (batman outline, anyone?). Just a simple electric clipper cut, number two on the back and sides and number four on the top. And in hot summers, or when going on holiday, an even simpler number two all over. Two minutes maximum, pensioner's rate, six quid please, thank you sir. (Ooh and thanks for the £1 tip, you cheapskate.)

Having spent years as pet owners, M and I are adept at grooming dogs, rabbits and guinea pigs, so we have a variety of battery-operated grooming clippers still lying around the house. And so it was with one of those that M sat me down on the stool and got to work. We did it outdoors so that the clippings wouldn't mess up the house or choke the shark, and in the hope that the excess hair would be used by birdies for nest building. Poor baby birds, imagine coming out of your shell expecting a cosy moss-lined nest, only to find you're surrounded by grey wispy hair? And smelling of Lacura apple shampoo, with pro-vitamin B5? No wonder they learn to fly early.

M tidied up the back and sides, which had really been annoying me, but she stopped short of going "over the top", so I still have enough hair on the top to allow me to comb it backwards, in a kind of quiff. If I only had some brylcreem I could wear it slicked back, like a 60s teddy boy, or a Chicago gangster. Is brylcreem still a thing? I'd forgotten all about it until now. When I was in school it was the epitome of cool, having your hair liberally brylcreemed and trying to look like Elvis in an attempt to impress the girls. Did it work? Not so much "burning love", more usually "lonesome tonight".

Today I should have been in the Northern Meeting Park, Inverness, for The Gathering. I mentioned The Gathering in the diary the other day, it's a one-day traditional music festival featuring some of Scotland's most popular musicians and bands. Like all festivals, it's a great day out and a good chance to meet up with friends and fellow music lovers, have some food and a few drinks. Like Glastonbury, but with slightly less mud.

Luckily, I already have a ticket for the 2021 Gathering, on Saturday May 29, so hope to see you there. Be sure to come and say hello. For those of you who don't know what I look like, I'll either be in the beer queue with my tongue hanging out, or the toilet queue with my legs crossed.

80

~~~

Social Distancing Diary – Day 77, a day of raw egg action
Today is Sunday May 31

Once again, up early and away for the long walk with M before the sun came out. Then the usual Sunday routine, breakfast, papers, Scotland on Sunday crossword. New word learnt today: "natant". Truly, every day's a school day.

For the first time since lockdown started, we had a couple of visitors in the garden for the afternoon.

Not much else to report, which is just as well because I ran out of space to tell you everything that happened yesterday.

I was nominated by a close friend to take part in the inane "egg, sugar, shot" challenge which is currently doing the rounds on Facebook here in the UK. Basically, it's a challenge in which you have to swallow a raw egg, followed by a spoonful of sugar, followed by a shot of whisky and make a donation to the NHS. And you have to film yourself doing it and post the movie on Facebook for all your friends to laugh at.

I've been saying for a few weeks that if I were nominated, I wouldn't do it. The thought of swallowing a raw egg was bad enough, but I was just as horrified by the prospect of eating sugar. M and I don't use sugar at all. We don't take it in any hot drinks, or on breakfast cereal. In fact we have some sugar in a glass jar in the house, but only in case any visitors need it, and it took some time yesterday to even locate a sugar bowl to put the sugar into for the challenge.

And I decided to use beer for the alcohol part of the challenge. I wasn't going to waste good malt whisky by throwing it down my throat like some Mexican bandido gulping his tequila. I hardly ever drink whisky, maybe only a couple of times a year, but when I do it has to be good quality malt (preferably from Speyside) and has to be sipped and savoured. Many years ago when I worked in the whisky industry, I remember being told by a senior, and highly experienced, colleague that a good malt should taste like "… sooking honey oot o' a bee's bum" . Now there's an image for you to carry away to your next cocktail party.

So there I was, egg, sugar and a can of John Smith's Yorkshire Bitter, seated at the patio table ready for my challenge. I had to get M to break the egg into a glass for me, I have no success in breaking eggs and keeping the yolks whole, every time I try to fry an egg the yolk always bursts and ends up like an omelette. I was wishing we'd kept one of the quail's eggs from a few weeks ago, they were tiny and would have been so easy to swallow. But no such luck, it had to be a proper egg. Sadly not from M Junior's chickens but from Lidl. I wonder where they keep their chickens, out the back of the shop, I expect. Luckily, when M cracked the egg into the glass, it turned out not to be a double yolker. That would have been one yolk too many.

With M doing the filming, I launched into my wee speech then tackled the raw egg. Down it went, in one big gulp. And almost came back up immediately, into the same glass. Fortunately it didn't, then I took the smallest spoon possible and filled it with the smallest amount of sugar possible, tipped in into my mouth and tried to swallow it. And made the huge mistake of putting the spoon back into the sugar bowl. Shock, horror! That might explain why I failed the practical exam when I applied to be catering manager at the Trump International Hotel. That, and my comb-over hairstyle.

Luckily we hadn't put very much sugar into the bowl so it wasn't too big a loss to throw it away. Down went the sugar, down went the beer, which was the most pleasant part of the operation, and that was the job done. Phew. If anyone has any more ideas for challenges please keep them to yourself.

81

~

Social Distancing Diary – Day 78, a day of inservice training

Today is Monday June 1. The start of a new week, and a new month.

This is an In-service Training day, or INSET, for Highland schools. In normal circumstances INSET days involve the kids having a day off school and the staff taking part in some sort of training, either in their own school or elsewhere. This time, of course, the kids get a day off from their Google classroom lessons while the staff have to do all their training online. Quite often, at the end of a training day, teachers get a chance to spend some time in their classroom to do some reorganising and rearranging, but today they're not allowed into the building. The only person allowed into M's school is M herself, and she has the head teacher's permission to shoot any staff who try to gain access. A little extreme, perhaps, so I don't think she'll be doing that. But I hear she's dug a system of trenches around the school and is patrolling at dawn and dusk, ready to repel any attacks.

Given a choice, I imagine most teachers would opt for centralised training because it gives them a chance to meet and interact with staff from other schools, to be taught by professional trainers, and –most importantly – there's usually a free lunch. Today I'm afraid their lunch will just be the same as any other day, home made and eaten in the same surroundings as in the past ten weeks. I know how they feel – I've eaten lunch in the same chair, at the same table, in the same company for 78 days in a row. With the only variety being provided by the newspaper headlines for the day. They're pretty boring these days, all "covid-19" this and "pandemic" that, and always full of doom and gloom. How I long for the days of entertaining headlines. "Freddie Starr ate my Hamster" would be a welcome relief. Although not to the hamster, obvs.

In England, today is the first day of primary schools reopening, with secondaries following suit in two weeks. Some parents will opt to keep their kids at home for a bit longer, but some will be very happy to hand them over after their home schooling experience. No doubt some families have taken to home learning like ducks to water, but I can imagine that for lots of frazzled parents the reverse is more accurate. "I'm not only your mother, I'm also your teacher" cuts no ice with a five-year-old who refuses to do sums unless the cat has to do them too, who insists that his "real" teacher allows him to draw on the walls, and who positively welcomes the threat of permanent exclusion.

Immediately after Popmaster I had a zoom meeting with some friends, which allowed me to show off my home-made haircut. Generally I think it was approved of, but there were some barely stifled giggles when I showed them the back of my head, upon which M had carved the letters P, R, A and T. How nice, after almost forty years, that she still thinks of me as Perfect, Romantic, And Tender.

After the meeting I cut the grass, which had grown alarmingly in the three days since I last did it. I've lowered the mower blade by one notch, so it's a little shorter than I usually have it. Maybe I should do the same with the hair clipper, to avoid any further carvings.

Yesterday the temperature reached 28°C, today by mid afternoon it was 30.8. Too hot for me, so no afternoon walk today. Instead, I went around the woods in the early evening which was a complete change from my usual activity of lounging in my armchair and snoozing through whatever M is watching on tv. Emmerdale and East Enders are both good to fall asleep to, but the best of all insomnia cures is Coronation Street. The first few notes of that distinctive signature tune and the first sight of that cat crouching on the pigeon loft roof, and I'm gone.

By the way, did you know that the Coronation Street cat was named Frisky? He lived to the age of 14 and was cremated, and his ashes were auctioned off. He wasn't so frisky after that.

Popmaster score: Round 1 – 9 points Round 2 – 12 points

82

∾

Social Distancing Diary – Day 79, a day of welcome rain

Today is Tuesday June 2, and at last a blessed relief from the heatwave we've had over the past few days. Maximum temperature in the back garden today was 15°C, half of what yesterday's was. The downside was that we had some light rain first thing, so I had to carry an umbrella on my morning walk. We have a variety of umbrellas but my favourite one was a present from M some years ago. Regular readers will know I'm a big motorcycle racing fan, and when a long, thin mystery package arrived, from a motorbike accessories company, I was delighted when it turned out to be an umbrella emblazoned with the MotoGP logo. Initially I had wondered whether M was buying me a motorbike one part at a time, and the handlebars were arriving first.

I've been lucky enough to have attended all classes of motorbike race meetings many times over the years, both in the UK and overseas. When I use my umbrella I'm reminded of one such event, I think it was in England, where umbrellas were on sale at £5 each. At one point in the weekend a huge storm blew in and there was torrential rain, and the price of umbrellas immediately doubled. So don't bother investing in the stock market. If you want to get rich quick, a supply of umbrellas and a wet weather front is all you need.

Today's rain was most appreciated by the vegetables in the garden, in particular the beetroots, which have been looking somewhat forlorn ever since they were planted out. I'm growing two varieties – "boltardy", which is the one which isn't doing so well, and "chiogga" which will grow into a striped beet with red and white rings. With a bit of judicious carving you can make your beetroot look like the international distress logo S O S in big red letters. And if you're lucky a St Bernard dog with a flask of brandy will arrive and save you from actually having to eat salad.

Speaking of stripy vegetables, clever M has raised (from seed) a tomato plant of the variety "tigerella". It's so called because the fruits will have red and yellow stripes, like a real tiger but slightly more approachable.

Now that her plant has reached a suitable size, she has foolishly handed it over to me so that I can pot it on and grow it alongside my two main tomatoes, "sweet aperitif" and "moneymaker". I can't imagine why she has so much faith in my tomato raising abilities. Out of six "shirley" tomatoes, I've successfully killed three of them already and the future's not looking too rosy for at least one of the survivors. I wouldn't go as far as to say I'm some sort of jinx, but if you're in hospital and waking up after your operation, you don't want my face to be the first one you see.

In the afternoon the rain was much heavier and the umbrella was even more necessary. Too miserable for a very long walk so today I've only done 18,000 steps and covered a mere 7.8 miles.

Since it was so wet I took the chance to have a hour of television watching after my afternoon walk, a rare luxury. Settled down to watch an episode of the Sopranos, and amongst all the shouting, threats and violence I began thinking: "My goodness, Tony Soprano has let himself go. And he badly needs a haircut".

Then I realised I'd pressed the wrong button and was watching Boris attending Prime Minister's Questions.

Popmaster score: Round 1 – 18 points Round 2 – 3 points.

83

～

Social Distancing Diary – Day 80, a day of varnishing

Today is Wednesday June 3. Eighty days! If I'd left on a round-the-world trip on Day One, instead of starting a diary, I could have been home by now.

Fence Man is back. Don't worry, he's not back to fix any problems with our fence, it's still standing and is much admired by passers-by. It keeps inquisitive small children out but, as predicted, it's not keeping El Gato out. He can clear it as easily as any Olympian show jumper, and he doesn't even have a horse.

Fence Man is working for the next door neighbours. They were impressed with the workmanship demonstrated by our fence, so they booked him to come and erect one for them too. There's a wee lane between our properties, which is used a lot by dog walkers and kids on bikes. Once Fence Man has finished there will be a nice wooden fence on either side of that lane so it will look much more attractive than the 40-year-old wire fences that were there up until a few weeks ago. I don't expect it will enhance the local property prices though, so it doesn't look as if we'll be putting the house on the market to make a huge profit any time soon. Anyway, where would we move to? Inverness, closer to Harry Gow's? Hmmm there's a thought.

Today I've been varnishing an otter. Now there's a sentence I never expected to write. But before you rush off and report me to the animal welfare organisations, I have to tell you it's not a real otter, but a garden ornament cast in stone. We actually have three of them, we got them a few years ago along with various other ornaments, and they've never been painted before. But this particular one sits at the front of the house, alongside the newly painted toadstool and a wee wooden planter shaped like a house, so M thought it looked kind of shabby and needed brightened up. She says I do too, but it will take more than a scrub with a wire brush and a coat of paint to brighten me up.

Anyway, we carried it round to my shed for its treatment (with some difficulty, because it's very heavy) and I scrubbed all the moss off it with a wire brush. And scrubbed most of the skin off my knuckles too which, although painful, is quite fortuitous because I was needing a new reason to avoid washing the dishes. I've milked the "berberis injury" for so long now, M was beginning to suspect I was just making up excuses. Whatever gave her that idea, I wonder?

Then once the otter was clean and moss-free, M set to with the paints. Terracotta colour for the log the otter is sitting on, and grey for the beast itself. And it looks good, but we were worried that rain might affect the paint so it needed to be varnished. After M came home from work yesterday she was despatched to Dingwall for a tin of outdoor varnish. I was secretly hoping for a tin of varnish AND a dream ring but sadly the baker was closed by that time. Or so she said, anyway.

And when she came home, she announced: "I've put the varnish in your shed". Which was a bit of a shock, because I thought that, being an expert painter, she'd apply the varnish herself. Obviously the implication was that I should do it. I mean, just because she works full time, cooks all the meals and does all the shopping, that's no excuse for leaving ME to do all the varnishing.

Anyway it's done now, with two coats, and once it's fully hardened the otter will be back in its proper place at the front of the house to amuse passers by, and scare small children.

Speaking of M cooking all the meals, I contributed to tonight's dinner. Yes, I made the pudding. Orange jelly and ice cream. Well actually Mr Lidl provided the ice cream but the jelly was all my own work, and I had to work with boiling water, even with my skinned knuckles.

Popmaster score: Round 1 – 3 points Round 2 – 9 points.

84

∾

Social Distancing Diary – Day 81, a day of not heading for the hills

Today is Thursday June 4. A very wet start to the day, but by the time I ventured out at 7am it had dried up and I completed my long walk without having to open my umbrella. By the end of the day the rain seems to have passed over and headed east. In the afternoon it was dry with sunny spells, but quite cool. Rather like myself.

M came home from the shop this morning with no newspapers. Disaster! The shop man had no explanation, simply that the papers hadn't turned up. This happens sometimes, if the roads are affected by snow or if they're closed for some other reason. So all through my morning walk, which takes almost two hours, I was anticipating having to use the internet to get my morning news. Or, even worse, endure daytime television.

But all was well in the end. When I got back from my walk, there were the papers, on the mat inside the front door. Clever M had gone back to the shop on her way to work and, discovering the papers had now arrived, popped back home and left them for me. Newspapers are a very important part of my life, not only in lockdown. I regularly read four a day, five on Wednesdays and Saturdays when M buys The Times, and today they range in size from 48 pages to 88 pages. It's a wonder I have time to do anything else.

Speaking of papers, today is paper recycling bin day. Every two weeks we put out our blue wheelie bin in which we place our paper, plastic and tins for recycling. When the bin man arrives, he always lifts the bin lid and has a cursory look inside, to ensure that there's no prohibited material in there. I always make sure that The Times is on the top of the pile, to give the bin man the impression that a posh person lives here. If he dug a little deeper and found The Sun or The Daily Mirror my reputation as a cultural icon would be ruined.

Today, if not for covid-19, would be the last day of exams in Scottish schools. Today's subjects are Mandarin and Cantonese, neither of which are taught in my school, so I would have been enjoying my first day off in six weeks. Or rather I wouldn't, because I had a booking to drive a minibus full of participants in the Duke of Edinburgh's Award Scheme. For overseas readers, this is an initiative whereby young people undertake various activities, including community work and life skills enhancement, but the part I'm involved with is the expedition element. Depending on whether the participants are going for a bronze, silver or gold award, they have to head to the hills, navigate a prescribed route and camp out for a number of nights. My job is to drive them to their starting point, which is invariably a remote and desolate spot, wave them goodbye and pick them up two, three or four days later at another remote and desolate spot. As long as they've read the map correctly.

And the most rewarding part of it for me is to see how happy they are to see me and my minibus when they complete their gruelling experience and arrive at the finish point, invariably exhausted, sweaty, soaked and insect-bitten. Luckily I don't have much of a sense of smell so I don't mind the aroma of wet children steaming quietly in the back of the bus, with their boots off for the first time in days.

Thursday night is zoom quiz night, with M Junior and friends. There's no theme this week because we've run out of ideas for costumes. Which is just as well because I've run out of cereal packets.

You will remember how delighted I was when I won last week. Tonight I reverted to my usual standard, and came a miserable last. Never mind, it's my turn to ask the questions next week and they'll be very, very hard.

Popmaster score: Round 1 – 6 points Round 2 – 12 points.

85

∽

Social Distancing Diary – Day 82, a day of weight loss and blood pressure gain

Today is Friday June 5 and I'm a mere shadow of my former self. My weekly weigh-in has revealed a further loss of two pounds in weight since last Friday. That's an amazing six pounds I've lost in the space of three weeks. I've had a week of sensible eating, no alcohol (until tonight), no snacks (no, not even a dream ring!). And I've walked more than fifty miles in the past seven days. If I'd done it in a straight line I'd be halfway to Perth by now.

It was dry but cool this morning, so M started up the washing machine before she left for work and when I came back from my long walk the washing was ready to be hung out. And as I was doing it, a cat came strolling casually down the garden path. Not El Gato, who runs away at the slightest approach, but a beautiful black and white puss who was very friendly. When he noticed me he took a detour and came across for a cuddle. I think he belongs to one of the neighbours, who happens to be a follower of this diary, so please tell him he's welcome to come for a hug any time. As long as he obeys the rules, which are: don't harass the birds, and don't poop in the vegetable plot. Those are the rules that apply to me, anyway.

We had a holiday booked for October and had paid the deposit, but the deadline for paying the balance was fast approaching. I knew that if it was cancelled by the travel company I would get credited with the deposit, but if I cancelled it myself I ran the risk of losing out. So it was with a great sense of relief I received an email from Trailfinders offering me various cancellation options. Rather than rebook for next year, we've decided to accept their offer of a credit note for the full value of the deposit, to be used against any future holiday, with, crucially, no expiry date. I've heard of airlines and other travel agents offering a similar deal, but with expiry dates of a year or less, and that puts pressure on the customer to book a holiday quickly. You might not even get your first choice of destination and that could be disastrous for anyone who ends up in Tenerife for two weeks when what they really wanted was a weekend in Dingwall.

Of course, with no travel this year I don't need travel insurance. I have an annual policy with a certain company, for worldwide travel for M and myself. As you might imagine, it ain't cheap. It doesn't expire until November so I thought there's no point in keeping it running for the next five months so I should cancel it. And surely I'd get a partial refund, wouldn't I? How naive was I?

First problem was actually contacting the company. As a regular customer (I have two non-travel policies as well as the travel one), I have a login and password to allow me to make changes online. At the first attempt I got a message "login or password incorrect". Second attempt: "If you've forgotten your password please click on this link", followed by: "a new password has been emailed to you". Sadly, and predictably, no such email has been received.

Blood pressure mounting, I gave up on the online thing and called the telephone "helpline". If ever a telephone number was misnamed it's this one. After the usual warnings about calls being recorded etc, and after pressing the appropriate button to speak to an operator, a recorded message tells the hapless customer that the lines are very busy and there's likely to be a wait of up to thirty minutes before your query can be answered. By this time the phone was overheating due to the steam coming out of my ears, so I hung up and reverted to email, as a last resort.

Simple email query: "please can I cancel my policy for the remainder of the term?" Simple email reply: "yes you can cancel the policy if you like, but there's no refunds because you're outwith the two-week cooling off period." Thanks, Insurance Company. I shan't be troubling you again for travel, car, home or any other insurance. Stick that in your cooling off period.

Popmaster score: Round 1 – 9 points Round 2 – 9 points.

86

~~

Social Distancing Diary – Day 83, a day of YouTube fame

Today is Saturday June 6, very wet in the morning but dried up as the day went on. M has Saturdays off so we have a joint walk, but because it was so wet we didn't do the full circuit, just an abbreviated version of around four miles. With umbrellas of course. And for a change we didn't meet any walkers, cyclists or joggers. And we didn't see any wildlife. All the animals were sheltering from the rain. Except fish, I suppose. And possibly frogs.

June the 6th is a day of two important anniversaries. Firstly, it was on this day in 1944 that Operation Overlord, otherwise known as the D-Day landings, took place. This invasion of Nazi-occupied France by allied forces heralded the start of the campaign to liberate Europe, and eventually led to victory almost a year later. Most of the troops involved in the landings were British, Canadian and American. However, troops of many other nationalities also took part, including Belgian, Czech, Danish, French, Greek, Polish and many more. I wonder how the generals managed to communicate their orders to these multilingual armies. No Google Translate in those days.

I suppose they reverted to that peculiarly British trait employed when speaking to foreigners – if they don't understand, keep on speaking in English but SHOUT LOUDER.

The other significant anniversary refers to Wednesday the 6th of June 1973. That was the date upon which I passed my car driving test. Second attempt, before you ask. I had held a full motorcycle licence since 1968 and always swore I'd never drive a car, but five Scottish winters on two wheels persuaded me that a nice tin box with a roof (and a heater) might not be so bad after all. Now, of course, I haven't driven for more than 80 days so I fear I'll have forgotten how. Maybe I need to book a few refresher driving lessons. Or maybe M will act as my instructor. After all, she's been issuing me with instructions for almost forty years.

Exciting news! I'm a YouTube star! I almost used the word "sensation", but that might be taking things a little too far. To explain, there's a popular band in Scotland named Tide Lines, who have recorded a new song called Taste the Rain which has a very catchy chorus. A couple of weeks ago, to create a bit of extra interest, they invited any of their followers to join in online, by singing the chorus (three times!) and filming themselves doing so. Unable to resist the opportunity to share in someone else's glory, I downloaded the backing track, got the headphones on, and chased M out for an hour while I filmed myself singing. And after several "takes" I emailed my film off to the band, in the firm belief that it would end up on the cutting room floor.

They had more than 150 submissions, most of which they were able to incorporate, and the result is a "Tide Lines Choir". And guess what? Somehow I made the cut and I'm in the band's official video. I can only imagine that they ended up with a tiny slot to fill, and thought: "let's stick that old fellow in, we'll mute his croaky voice and no-one will notice".

But don't get too excited, because if you blink you'll miss me. Because of the huge response there are about fifty of us on screen at any one time, some in bigger frames than others, and we're each visible for only a short time. Tucked away near the edge, in a postage stamp-sized frame, I had to use a magnifying glass in order to locate myself. So I defy any of you to spot me amongst the younger, more glamorous singers surrounding me.

It's a good song though, so do please have a listen. And if you're watching it on YouTube I suggest you look away from 2:18 until 2:26. I'd hate to give you nightmares.

87

~

Social Distancing Diary – Day 84, a day of cheese and wine

Today is Sunday June 7, and this morning was rain-free. And, unusually, cat-free. No sign of El Gato when we got up so we expected him to be on the doorstep when we got back from our morning walk, but no, he didn't appear until four o'clock in the afternoon. With no explanation for absence. We suspect he was out on the town last night and met a lady cat.

It wasn't a crow-free morning, however. For the second time in recent days Percy and his pals have broken the birds peanut feeder by hanging on it and swinging wildly until it came off its hook. A few days ago the same thing happened and I mended it with copious amounts of superglue, but today it came apart again. So it's now in the shed, in intensive care, been glued to within an inch of its life and clamped together until the glue dries. Tomorrow I shall hang it out again, but I'm not optimistic that the crows will leave it alone. Percy is the ringleader, at first he came alone but has now gathered a large gang of followers. In mafia terms, he's definitely the Tony Soprano of the crow world.

Eighty-four days! That's the end of my twelve weeks of self isolation, as recommended by Nicola for we so-called vulnerable people. So that means I can start going back out into society tomorrow. The trouble is that I have absolutely no desire to go anywhere near society. I've become so used to living in my own wee bubble of home/garden/local walks, I can't imagine why I would want to go anywhere, not even Inverness or Dingwall.

Am I turning into a hermit? Should I start wearing rags and living in a cave? I'm already halfway there with the rags, been living in micro fleeces and sports trousers and haven't worn smart clothes for weeks.

Speaking of smart clothes, M has bought me a nice present. A couple of weeks ago, I admired a pair of smart brown brogue shoes in one of her mail order catalogues and, after only a small amount of hinting (well, quite a lot actually) she sent away for them and they arrived the other day. And you'll remember she bought me a pair of jeans (with elasticated waistband!) a few weeks ago, so if not for M, I wouldn't have anything decent to wear.

So maybe I will go out tomorrow, in my new jeans and shoes, and drive to Dingwall for a walk along the street. Although there's always a danger of coronavirus, there's a bigger danger in Dingwall. A walk along the High Street will inevitably involve passing Harry Gow's, and there will be dream rings in the window. Do I have the willpower to just walk past, or will I be tempted?

Today's lunch was special. Lunch for me is almost always a simple sandwich, with corned beef, tuna or whatever sandwich filling is in the fridge. Today's was cheese and lettuce. What's special about that, I hear you ask? Well, for the first time this year we enjoyed the fruits of our labours, in that the lettuce was home-grown from seed. Sown at the same time as the carrots, and grown in a window box instead of the vegetable patch, the lettuce was well established before the carrots even came through the ground. The variety is little gem, if you're interested, and there are a few more nearly ready for harvesting so it looks like we'll be having plenty healthy salads this summer. Which will be good for my weight control, although not as much fun as my favourite diet of burgers, chips and beer.

Lovely Italian neighbour sent her daughter round today, to pop a bottle of wine on our doormat just as a thank you for keeping an eye on her. And she'd already given us a batch of freshly made scones earlier in the morning. Typical Italian generosity, combined with a love of food and drink. It's just as well I live here and not next door, or I'd be the size of Pavarotti. Mama mia!

88

〜〜

Social Distancing Diary – Day 85, a day of going to town

Today is Monday June 8, and M is back to work so I had my morning walk on my own. It was down to 3°C overnight so quite chilly at first, but soon warmed up.

Yesterday I told you that I was a little wary of going away from home, amongst people for the first time in nearly three months. Well, today I took the bull by the horns and drove to Dingwall. M had a letter she wanted me to post, and instead of just walking down to my local postbox in the village, I thought it would be a good incentive for me to go to town and post it there. And it was a good chance for me to dress smartly for a change, so I cast off my scruffy polo shirt and working trousers and replaced them with a smart polo shirt and jeans. And as a special treat I wore my brand new brown brogues, which are nice and shiny. When I looked in the mirror I didn't recognise the fashion icon staring back at me. At first I thought: "What's Daniel Craig doing in my bedroom?" Then when I saw the hairstyle I thought: "Nah, it's Bob Geldof".

I must say though, it wasn't a comfortable experience. I deliberately parked at the wrong end of town so as to force myself to walk the whole length of the High Street, which must be around a quarter of a mile. And it felt like a scene from some sort of futuristic film. Almost all of the shops are closed and there are staff members standing guard outside the banks and the chemists to control numbers of customers. Kind of like nightclub bouncers, except they let you in without a tie.

Surprisingly there were quite a few people on the street, during my walk I counted forty or so, in groups and singles, of all age groups. Which is probably about right for Dingwall on a Monday, regardless of lockdown. I've been used to meeting only occasional people in ones and twos on my walks, so it was a big shock being amongst such a crowd. And what surprised me was that no-one was wearing a mask, except me. No wonder the bank lady withdrew into the doorway as I passed.

Now that we're firmly into summer, my winter pansies have finally given up flowering. They've been on display in my wooden planter (made to look like a wee white cottage) since autumn, and have survived everything that winter threw at them. Which, quite honestly, wasn't much. We haven't had a proper winter here for quite a few years now, no heavy snowfalls and no serious frost. Our winter season nowadays seems to be predominantly warm and damp which is ok in the garden, but not so much in the bedroom.

Anyway, the poor pansies have become straggly and weak, so I've brought them into the back garden for a period of rest and recovery. They'll get a good trimming and I'll find a cool spot for them to spend a few months before going back out on display. I might even plant them in a spare area of the vegetable plot and maybe they'll show the carrots how to grow. The carrot variety is flyaway, I suspect they should have been called shy away.

Had a nice zoom meeting this morning with former colleagues, some of whom are still working in schools. Some are going back into school briefly this week, some not for a week or so yet. It must be a nightmare for head teachers trying to work out timetables for the new "blended learning", especially in the bigger schools. Imagine trying to accommodate a thousand pupils, perhaps a third or a quarter of whom are in school on any one day, juggling with transport arrangements and catering facilities. Not to mention the whole question of ensuring social distancing in corridors and play areas. And, of course, toilets. How will they control numbers using the toilets? Will a teacher be stationed outside every cubicle keeping a register of every child who enters, and issuing one sheet of toilet paper? Or maybe they'll make them go in alphabetical order, which is good news for Andrew Adam but not so good for Zelda Zablowski. Poor cross-legged Zelda, I hope she doesn't catch cold because she'll be afraid to sneeze.

Popmaster score: Round 1 – 3 points Round 2 – 15 points.

89

∽

Social Distancing Diary – Day 86, a day of remembering yesterday

Today is Tuesday June 9, and there are a couple of things I forgot to tell you about yesterday. Firstly, my fitness regime. I was astounded last night when I checked my fitbit and found that I'd walked 24,000 steps, and a distance of twelve miles. This is because I did the long walk on my own in the morning, and again with M when she came home from school. Plus my half mile in Dingwall High Street and the usual pottering around at home. So today I made a special effort not to exercise quite so much, apart from my morning walk. I decided not to accompany M after school, which was quite wise as it turned out because shortly after she left the rain came on. OK, so I had to rush out and take in the washing, but it was still easier than walking five miles in the rain.

And the other thing relates to Harry Gow and his famous dream rings. Some of you have been asking whether I bought myself a dream ring during my trip to Dingwall. Well, I'm very proud to say I didn't. But before you rush to congratulate me on my self control, I have to confess that I did actually approach the shop (just to take a look in the window, you understand!) and found to my dismay that Harry only opens his Dingwall shop from Tuesdays to Saturdays. It's probably just as well, because I'm sure my willpower would have crumbled at the sight of a dream ring calling to me through the window, like some high-cholestrol, full cream, sugary mermaid tempting sailors to their doom.

Anyway, what happened today? Well it was a busy old day, dry in the morning with rain forecast for the afternoon so immediately after breakfast I got busy in the garden, with a break for Popmaster of course. Got the grass cut and the edges strimmed, after which I went to top up the strimmer fuel and found that I'd run out. My strimmer runs on two-stroke fuel, which means I have to mix petrol (gasoline for my American friends!) and oil, in the correct proportions. And those proportions, for my current strimmer, are 50:1, ie fifty parts of petrol to one of oil. Some tricky mental arithmetic was required to work it out. I passed my O'Grade Arithmetic in the days of pints, quarts and gallons, so I struggle to get to grips with litres, centilitres and millilitres. I always thought these last ones were wee beasties with lots of legs.

My old strimmer had a different mixture, it was 25:1, and I remember studying the instructions and getting confused, and reading it as 25%, which is outrageously oily. Anyway, I mixed the fuel, filled the tank and started the machine. And was immediately enveloped in a huge choking cloud of black smoke, which rose into the air and threatened to block out the sun. And there were repercussions. All flights were grounded throughout Europe, and the American space exploration programme was put on hold because they couldn't even see the moon, far less land on it.

But no oily problems with my next job of the day, which was to trim some ivy which grows up an arch at a corner of the house. It needs trimmed two or three times a year because, although it has a perfectly good wooden arch to climb up, it's determined to reach out to the house and cling to the wall. Trimming it has always been a difficult and dangerous job involving a shaky stepladder, an electric hedge trimmer with an extension cable and a constant flow of expletives, in various languages.

And, for the neighbours, it's been a great source of amusement. I'm sure they take bets on how long it will take me to fall off the ladder, slice the hedge trimmer cable or (my favourite trick) cut through the washing line which runs close to the arch.

No such entertainment today, however. I've invested in a cordless, long reach hedge trimmer so I can do the entire job with both feet firmly on the ground. And in a fraction of the time and without any swearing. And the washing line survived the operation, which is just as well, because my "Atlas For Men" underwear was hanging on it at the time. With extra pegs for added security.

Popmaster score: Round 1 – 9 points Round 2 – 6 points.

90

∽

Social Distancing Diary – Day 87, a day of staying indoors

Today is Wednesday June 10, and a bleak, wet day it has been. Morning walk had to feature the umbrella, which means I wasn't able to take my walking pole. I don't really need it now because my ankle (touch wood!) has been fine recently. It seems that simply going for long walks is a much better cure for ankle problems than all that painful physiotherapy. Although I have to admit that maybe the weight loss is helping too.

The plants which I ordered to keep the cat out of my garden arrived today. There are twelve wee plug plants, which seem to have survived their traumatic journey reasonably well, so I hope they will thrive a little better than the Shirley tomatoes, only four of which are still alive. I've transplanted them into cell trays, using good quality compost, and placed them in M's mini greenhouse. The variety is Coleus "scaredycat" and, in theory at any rate, emit an odour which discourages cats from doing in the garden what bears do in the woods.

Until they're strong enough to get planted out along the perimeter of the veg garden the temporary fence will have to stay in place. It's doing a great job of deterring the cat, but it makes it awkward for me to get easy access so I've been neglecting my weeding. Also, I'll need in at some point to thin the carrots too, but at the rate they're growing I don't think I'll need to do that until Christmas.

And speaking of the cat, El Gato was being elusive again today. M was worried about him because he didn't appear at breakfast time, and still hadn't turned up by the time she left for school. Yesterday he spent the whole day hanging around our back garden, but today he didn't appear until 11.36am. I tried telling him he'd missed breakfast, but he refused to go away unless I fed him, so I was obliged to give him brunch.

Because it was such a miserable wet day, apart from the morning walk and the Coleus planting I spent most of my time indoors. Luckily Wednesday is one of the days M buys me The Times, so that helped pass an hour or so. And of course there's the crossword, which usually takes a day or more. I haven't done much of it today, but I've photocopied it for tomorrow. Saturday's one was a real stinker, I found it absolutely impossible and only got three or four answers before reverting to Mr Google, and even he struggled. I've checked the Times Crossword Help Forum online, and was relieved to see that I wasn't the only one who had trouble on Saturday.

Maybe The Times is a little too advanced for me after all and I should stick to my natural intellectual level. I wonder if they still have a puzzle page in the Beano?

Tomorrow night it's my turn to host the weekly zoom quiz, so I spent most of this morning preparing the questions. It's surprising how much time it takes to make up a quiz, but at least I'll be the one asking the questions, so will be spared the indignity of coming last.

Also tomorrow night, we're looking forward to seeing M Junior on the telly. The BBC programme "Landward" features, as the name suggests, Scottish rural affairs and local interest stories, and Farmer J is featured in one of the items tomorrow night. We've seen a trailer for the show, and you'll be able to spot M Junior feeding her chickens. And Dog F, of course, who is a regular star of stage and television. She's been on the STV News, on BBC's Countryfile show and even made a celebrity guest appearance live on stage, in Blairgowrie Players' pantomime in December.

If you'd like to tune in, it's on the BBC Scotland HD channel, Thursday 8pm UK time.

Overseas readers may need to catch it online after the event, on BBC iplayer. And Farmer J speaks in a broad Perthshire accent, so you may feel the benefit of subtitles.

Popmaster score: Round 1 – 9 points Round 2 – 6 points.

91

∽

Social Distancing Diary – Day 88, a day of refund successes

Today is Thursday June 11. Even wetter than yesterday, I needed not only the umbrella but also my waterproof overtrousers for my morning walk. On the plus side, the weather kept everyone else away, so I didn't meet any walkers, cyclists or joggers until I was almost home. Was passed by a couple of cars though, on the single track road, which meant having to go in amongst the long wet grass at the roadside to let them past. And when the bin lorry came I had to get even further off the road, which was a good test for the waterproofing of my boots. Can't have my nice new socks getting wet, can we?

Oh yes, my new socks. I haven't told you about them yet. Last weekend an offer in Saturday's Times caught my eye. A pack of gents' socks, brightly coloured and made of cotton with non-elasticated tops. Hopefully more comfortable than the nylon ones I'm used to, which don't last very long before my big toe pokes through. I thought they'd be ideal for long distance walking, and hopefully hard wearing. And the deciding factor was that they were on special offer.

Always one for a bargain, M got on to the website and ordered a pack, and they came within a couple of days, as promised. And very comfortable they are too. There are six pairs in the pack, which is almost enough for a full week, Monday to Saturday. I suppose that means I shall have to do without socks on a Sunday. I won't be able to wear my walking boots, so I'll have to go round the woods in my flip flops, like some latter day version of Gandhi, but with more hair.

Now that our October holidays have been officially cancelled, and my Trailfinders deposit is safe and sound, there were a couple of related bookings I needed to cancel. Since my record of squeezing refunds out of reluctant companies isn't great, I took a deep breath before getting on the phone. But thanks to my strategy of acting like a pathetic, doddery old fool it was largely successful. Two out of three calls had a positive result, so my success rate is 66% which, although not perfect, at least beats my quiz winning rate by a mile.

I had booked Glasgow Airport car parking for the full two weeks, at a cost of £73 which was a special advance rate and non refundable so I was expecting a firm "no" when I called to cancel. And the answer was: "no, sorry we can't do refunds, but we'll give you a credit note towards your next booking". Fair enough, I thought, but how long will it be valid for, and will it be for the full amount? Happily, the answer was that it's valid until the end of December 2021 and the value isn't the £73 I paid, but a full £75! So I'm two pounds up on the deal and even if we don't need airport car parking next year I'm sure some of our family and friends can use it. For a reasonable fee, of course.

Next, an overnight stay in a hotel at the beginning of the holiday. Not just any old hotel, but the Hilton at Schiphol Airport in Amsterdam which is quite posh, but no expense spared for my dear wife. Also, all the cheaper ones were sold out.

Again, special rate, and again not cancellable but when I explained the circumstances they said that the booking could be cancelled without any penalty. So no profit this time, but no loss either.

And the final booking was for a hotel at Glasgow Airport at the end of the trip, so we could have a night's rest before driving up the road. And this time I didn't get a definite "no", but I got a "not yet, but try again nearer the time", which is pretty much what I expected. And it's only a quarter of the cost of the Amsterdam Hilton, so even if I have to write it off it won't break my heart, or my wallet, too much.

So the moral of the story is, don't be afraid to phone and ask for a refund. And if you play the part of a silly old duffer you'll have a good chance of success.

Popmaster score: Round 1 – 12 points Round 2 – 18 points.

92

Social Distancing Diary – Day 89, a day of garden activity

Today is Friday June 12, a beautiful morning and the first walk for a few days without an umbrella, or even a jacket. And when I came home it was weekly weigh-in time. According to the scales I've lost another pound since last Friday so I have three weeks left in which to lose another three pounds. I'm really not sure this is achievable, my rate of loss is bound to slow down shortly and there's always the danger of temptation by dream ring. Get thee behind me, Harry Gow.

I ran out of space before I could tell you a couple of things that happened last night. Firstly, we had our usual Zoom quiz at 7pm, with M Junior and a couple of friends. Partners are allowed to join in so Farmer J was on M Junior's team. And they won the competition assisted by Dog F, who eagerly joined in –presumably hoping for some sheepdog questions.

And an hour later we saw them again, on BBC Scotland's Landward programme. Farmer J gave us a little insight into what he's up to on the farm, and then the highlight of the show was a nightly ceremony called "chicken bedtime". This involves M Junior, assisted by Dog F, leading the chickens to their coop at the end of the day. All she says is: "come on, then", and the chickens follow her as obediently as a row of well disciplined schoolgirls following Miss Jean Brodie.

Today was a busy day for me. And for M too, of course, because she was at work preparing her schools for the staff returning in a week or two. But while she was doing that I was planting out the last of the broccoli and brussels sprouts, into the final space in the veg plot. So we now have three rows of broccoli and three of sprouts, and there's only two of us, so by the time we've eaten all that we'll be bursting with health. Or gas. Also, thanks to broccoli's high iron content M will be able to decorate me with fridge magnets.

I also cut the grass, second time this week, and left the clippings on the ground. I'm convinced that it helps the grass to grow thicker so I don't mind cutting it twice a week. It's quite therapeutic walking behind the mower, and as a bonus the vibrations of the mower increase my daily step count so I can feel even more virtuous.

I've recycled a couple of old biscuit tins, one with the Rich Tea Biscuit pattern and the other with the Tetley Tea logo, both typically British brands. A month or so ago I bored holes in their bases, filled them with compost and sowed some lobelia seeds then sat back to see what would grow. And as it happened, nothing did. Luckily M had some spare seedlings which she was willing to give me, so I've planted these in the tins and they're outside now, looking quite good. I can just imagine what the neighbours are saying: "By heck, Sandy's taking this diet very seriously. Not only has he stopped eating biscuits, he's even thrown out the tins".

And the final garden related thing I did was to replant my wee wooden house. You'll remember I took the winter flowering pansies out of it on Day 85 because they had stopped flowering and were in need of a rest. Well I've trimmed all their dead parts and popped them into a window box at the end of the shed so they can rest all summer until it's time for them to flower again. Kind of like hedgehogs hibernating all winter but not quite so prickly.

And the pansies' place has been taken by nasturtiums, which M grew from an old packet of seeds given away as a free gift with a gardening magazine last year. Nasturtiums are always reliable, easy to grow and prolific flowering. These are an all-yellow variety and just on the point of flowering so my public display includes a grey otter on a red base, red toadstools with white spots and a white house with yellow flowers. If you spotted that lot on your way home from the pub you'd think you were hallucinating and you'd probably never drink again.

Popmaster score: Round 1 – 21 points Round 2 – 21 points.

93

～

Social Distancing Diary – Day 90, a day of environmental phenomena

Today is Saturday June 13, and ninety days since this diary started. Shockingly, that's almost thirteen weeks, or a quarter of a year.

The weekend is upon us again. This means that M is at home all day, so we had our usual Saturday morning walk together on a dull morning which brightened up nicely as the day went on. Unlike me. I'm pretty dull at the start of every day, and still dull (even duller, if that's possible) at the end.

And like every other Saturday for the past thirteen weeks, M bought me The Times as my weekend treat. It takes me a couple of hours to read, and a couple of days to do the crossword. Although I must say I completed Wednesday's crossword in record time, and only had to revert to Mr Google once. I'd never heard of "Proconsul" before, but it turns out that it was a term for a high ranking official in Roman times, not some sort of kid's computer gaming device.

The "environmental" reference in today's heading involves two incidents. Firstly we've been coated in some sort of yellow peril. It seems to be caused by pollen in the air being washed down by recent rain and then drying up, leaving everything covered in a nasty sticky yellow powder. Our cars are coated with it, likewise window sills, and even the outside doors have turned yellow. And it's not easy to get rid of, a simple wipe with a damp cloth simply spreads it around. The only way is to wash it with warm soapy water then rinse. If you need help, just follow the instructions on the shampoo bottle.

This yellow dust inspired M to wash the windows, which were very obscured. I could hardly keep an eye on what the neighbours were up to, which, rather than plain nosiness, I see as my civic duty. But everything was so yellow , it was like looking out at a sandstorm in the Sahara rather than a quiet street in a Ross-shire village. I was sure I saw a miniature camel passing the window, but it turned out to be El Gato coming for his lunch break.

Which was lucky for him, because I had made sardines on toast for my own lunch (see how healthy my diet is!) and I'd left a spare one for him. So instead of a boring old cat food pouch from Poundstretcher he had a nice tasty sardine from Lidl. I'm very happy to share my food with him, but if I ever get a dream ring he ain't getting a taste of that.

The other natural phenomenon is fungus related. No, not a nasty dose of athlete's foot but an invasion of small mushroom-like growths in our central garden area. This is the area, you might remember, where the wall had fallen down during winter and was repaired away back on Day 23. To refresh your memory, it's a central bed surrounded by cobble stones, with some roses in containers and a couple of bird baths, and the whole area is top dressed with gravel. And in the middle are a couple of stumps from lime trees which were cut down years ago, and a taller one which is Percy's favourite perching spot.

Overnight, a huge number of tiny mushrooms has appeared, crowded together in big clumps, and spread all over the area. They're like a gathering of mini woodland creatures from some children's cartoon show, I almost expect them to come to life after dark, and start marching around the garden. I don't want anyone marching around my garden after dark, except myself of course, so I got stuck in with a dutch hoe and scraped them all up. M warned me not to touch them with my bare hands in case they're poisonous, but her warning came too late. My hands were already contaminated with their slimy spores so I had to rush indoors and get them washed, to the tune of "Happy Birthday To You" as prescribed by Boris.

It could have been worse, at least I only have two hands to wash. Just think of the poor teacher supervising a 20-strong infant class washing their hands before lunch. That's a lot of happy birthdays but no presents.

94

~~~

Social Distancing Diary – Day 91, a day of online music and confusing instructions

Today is Sunday June 14, and this weekend I should have been at the Keith Festival. For those who don't know, this is one of the main Scottish traditional music festivals of the year, and takes place in the town of Keith in Banffshire. Or at least it used to be in Banffshire, until local government reorganisation in 1975 moved it into the Moray Council area.

Keith describes itself as "The Friendly Town", and indeed it is very welcoming, especially during the festival weekend. And especially in the various pubs, many of which feature live music sessions. I usually manage to go along on the Saturday and enter the Bothy Ballad competitions. (Overseas readers may wish to refer to Google!)

This year, of course, the event has been cancelled due to Covid-19, along with every other event on the 2021 calendar. However the enterprising folks who run the festival were determined that it should go ahead in some form, so they arranged a whole weekend's worth of online events, concerts, singing sessions, and even a dance. Yes, a dance! For those of us stuck at home, so we could waltz around the living room. I tried it, but found that it's not easy doing a slow foxtrot while avoiding the sofa, and wearing a worn-out pair of carpet slippers.

So this weekend I've spent a considerable amount of time watching and listening to the online events. It's been great seeing and hearing a variety of performers, many of whom I know and others whom I haven't met yet, but it's not quite the same as being in the room with them. And although I can sit with a dram and join in with the choruses I can't hear anyone else joining in. And luckily for them, no-one else can hear me.

I've had to place an emergency order with Mr Argos. He, along with Mr Google and Mr Amazon, is one of my best pals and someone I turn to in times of need. We have a device called a projecting alarm clock, which sounds painful, if not downright dangerous. But really what it does is project the time in big red characters on to the bedroom ceiling so that I always know what time it is when M kicks me in the middle of the night in an attempt to stop me snoring.

Sadly, it's begun to give up the ghost. One by one, its LED characters are failing, and so the display can be very misleading. The eight now looks like a three, and the seven like a one, so we never know whether it's time to get up and feed the cat, or time to roll over and carry on snoring. And getting kicked.

Fortunately Mr Argos is a very helpful sort of fellow, and he's delivering a replacement tomorrow afternoon between 1pm and 6pm. Or, according to our clock, between 1pm and 1pm. Then we can have all the fun of setting it up, which leads me on to the sorry tale of the wireless headphones...

I use my laptop constantly to listen to music (this weekend's Keith Festival is a classic example), and for years I've been restricted by the length of the headphone cable and forced to remain seated in front of the computer. I thought I should move with the times and invest in a set of wireless headphones so I could sit and relax in my armchair while listening to my favourite singers. And Mr Amazon delivered a set at lunchtime today. Which was fine until I began reading the instruction booklet, which is printed in characters so small that neither M nor I could read them without a magnifying glass, like a latter-day Holmes and Watson examining a crime scene.

And indeed a crime scene would be less confusing. Here's a couple of examples: "At this Bluetooth headset can be find in the state", and "...then your favourite melodious singing softly sounded".

I suspect I'll be enlisting Mr Google's help with the setting up, but in the meantime I fear I shall be remaining firmly attached (by umbilical cord) to the headphone socket for some time yet.

95

〜

Social Distancing Diary – Day 92, a day of damp grass and a wee windfall

Today is Monday June 15, and a damp start meant I needed a jacket on my morning walk. But as well as being damp it was uncomfortably warm, so it was a greasy blob who arrived home two hours later and was glad to get into a cool shower.

I was lamenting the wet start, because I had planned to cut grass today. The forecast for the week is very wet so I thought today was my only chance. By mid afternoon it had dried slightly, and so against my better judgement I cut it while it was still slightly damp. And that's it done, so it can rain if it likes, but knowing my luck we'll have a heatwave.

Got a nice wee boost to my bank balance today. In a normal year I'd expect to get paid by the SQA for organising and supervising this year's exams, but as you know, all exams were cancelled this year so no big fat cheque for me. There's a significant amount of preparatory work which Chief Invigilators have to carry out in advance of the exams, some of it several weeks in advance, and I had hoped the SQA would pay us an allowance in respect of that. However, when Scot Gov announced the cancellation of the exams, the SQA's initial reaction was: "If you don't do the exams, you don't get paid". Throughout Scotland, schools resounded with the sound of toys being thrown out of Chief Invigilators' prams. We're more easily upset than the pupils, and just as tearful if we don't get our own way.

But it looks like the complaining has had an effect, and someone in authority has had a change of heart, because a few weeks ago I was invited to submit a claim for any hours incurred in exam preparation. I sent in a modest claim and today payment has arrived. The taxman took a big chunk of it away of course, but it was decent of the SQA to recognise our hard work, and the toys are now back in the pram. Until next year, at least.

Good news too, on the tomato front. Both my sweet aperitif and moneymaker varieties have flowered well, and the latter has a good crop of small green fruits already. Also, my shirleys and M's tigerellas are strong enough now to be planted out, my plan is to grow them as outdoor varieties against a south facing wall, and hope for a decent spell of sunshine this summer. The only danger with growing them outdoors is that they'll be accessible to the birds so they're liable to be pecked. Or pooped on. Or both.

To my horror, in the middle of Popmaster today, someone rang the door bell, and that's my excuse for today's pathetic scores. Although, on playing back the recording, it turns out that my scores would have been pathetic anyway.

When M came home from school today she brought a broken trophy for me to fix. It's a figure of a footballer who should have been on a plinth, but wasn't because he had become detached. An easy fix, with a wee nut and bolt and a drop of glue, he's now standing proudly on his plinth again. It's a very nice trophy, and would look good on my sideboard so I was tempted to keep it for myself. Any visitors could admire it, and I could regale them with tales of my footballing skills. However my street cred would soon be destroyed when they read the plate on the front: "Under 12s Football 2018".

I suppose I could always claim that "under twelve" refers to my weight in stones, not my age. But even that would require a considerable stretch of the imagination.

Popmaster score: Round 1 – 3 points Round 2 – 3 points.

96

∾

Social Distancing Diary – Day 93, a day of venturing away from home

Today is Tuesday June 16 and it stayed dry most of the day. I had a very pleasant walk in the morning, no jacket, hat or umbrella required. And at 3pm the BBC weather page on my phone assured me it was raining, but a look out of the window revealed a rain-free afternoon. I could easily have delayed yesterday's damp grass cutting until today because the rain didn't come on until 8pm.

When I awoke this morning, I knew immediately what time it was, thanks to the new projecting clock device. There on the ceiling, in big red characters, was 06:20. The clock was delivered yesterday, and installed by M last night, with the minimum of fuss. I kept well away from the operation because my record of installing new devices (see Sunday's headphone saga) is fraught with difficulties and immoderate language.

M was already up, of course, had been to the shop for the papers, had fed the cat and brought me my tea in bed. Every working day for the twenty-two years up until I retired, I had brought M her morning tea in bed, then since I retired the situation has reversed. Except at exam times of course, when I have to be up early and away by half past seven. I like to be in school early to build up some aggression so I can put the fear of death into the pupils. Who am I kidding? I'm much more scared of them that they are of me.

Lots of staff are back in schools this week, preparing classrooms and resources ready for the day when kids return in August, and sorting out the very complicated admin details. Timetables, accommodation, catering and transport are all causing nightmares for head teachers and staff. So because some of my colleagues are back at work, we haven't had our customary zoom meeting this week. Zoom has been a real boon during lockdown, it gives us a chance to have a proper face to face chat without the risk of being in the same room. And gives everyone a chance to have a laugh at my ridiculous hairstyle. Remember Hagrid in the Harry Potter films? I'm like his older, smaller, less handsome brother.

Also because of school staff going back, there's no zoom quiz this week. One of our regular participants is a head teacher, and M Junior is herself a teacher, although she's on maternity leave now. The zoom quiz is another thing which has helped offset the monotony of lockdown, always good fun and usually challenging. Sometimes very challenging indeed. According to my calculations we had a total of nine quizzes, only one of which was won by me. That's an eighty-nine percent failure rate or, if

I was a politician looking for your vote, a massive 11.1111% success rate.

Today I was very brave and went out in the car. It's only my second time away from home, apart from my walks of course, but I needed petrol for my lawnmower so I drove into Dingwall and filled up my fuel can at the self service pump. And afterwards instead of heading straight home I decided to have a wee drive around, just for pleasure and to give the car a chance to have a proper warm-up, and blow the cobwebs out of the exhaust pipe.

In spite of my fears about forgetting how to drive, I managed to navigate safely a circular route of around ten miles, part of it on the main A9, which is the major north-south route through the highlands. Quite a lot of traffic around, much of which is commercial, especially delivery vans. It seems that online shopping has become more popular than ever during lockdown. Even in our wee cul-de-sac delivery vans make regular appearances, and we all rush to our windows to see which household is getting the delivery.

Today's one was a pack of printer ink from Amazon which I ordered at the weekend, so today's score is Thomsons one, neighbours nil.

Popmaster score: Round 1 – 6 points Round 2 – 15 points.

97

Social Distancing Diary – Day 94, a day of progress in technology

Today is Wednesday June 17, a very wet start and a good soaking during the morning walk. As soon as I got home I had to change all my clothes and put them in the wash, although I wasn't able to get them hung out to dry until early afternoon.

Two exciting new things arrived today. Firstly the postie brought my credit card bill, which wasn't one of the exciting things, and a brand new internet hub from BT, which was. Apparently I'm being converted to fibre, which I thought would be good news for my digestive system, because we all need more fibre, don't we? And how kind of BT to supply it, I didn't know they'd diversified into healthcare.

However, closer inspection of the package revealed that it's not my digestive tract, but my broadband connection which is being converted from copper to fibre. According to BT, I'm going to have a "Switch Over Day" upon which this conversion will take place, but they're not telling me when it is, so I have to install the new hub TODAY! Never one to question the voice of authority, I duly installed the new device and packaged up the old one ready to return to BT. Just as soon as I've plucked up the courage to enter the Post Office.

I haven't been inside a shop for three months so it will be a nerve wracking step, but just as I forced myself to go to the petrol station yesterday I'll need to force myself to get this parcel posted. It's not the process I'm wary of, it's in case any of the other customers breathes on me. I wonder if I can get from the front door to the counter, hand over the parcel, get the receipt and get out the door without breathing? I wish I'd paid more attention to the breathing exercises during my twenty-five years singing in choirs. Is it too late to start now?

And once the hub was up and running it was time to change the login and password details on every device in the house. And there's a lot of them. My laptop, M's laptop, our joint tablet, M's personal tablet, my smart phone, my spare phone, my spare spare phone, the printer and my kindle. Everything but the kitchen sink. Phew I had earned my coffee break by the time all that was done, but in the middle of my coffee break I realised I'd forgotten to include the telly. And the telly is very important because without broadband there's no catch up tv, and without catch up tv there's no Sopranos. However I'm happy to report that we're all fixed up now, and I'm fully connected to Tony and his chums. So if anyone causes me any aggro I can scare them off by saying, truthfully, that I have a mafia connection.

And today's other exciting delivery came at 9.30am – a new laptop! My poor old one took ill in February, spent a few days in computer hospital, and was discharged with a new hard drive. Oh, and an external mouse attached because its mouse pad had given up the ghost. So I've been labouring since then with a slow elderly laptop with an annoying external mouse, so I decided to invest in a replacement. This one is bang up to date (although I hope it doesn't go bang!) and has a 17.3" screen, which is a real treat for my poor eyesight, which should have been tested in March, just as Specsavers went into lockdown.

A couple of interesting hours were spent getting the new laptop set up, but the whole process was remarkably trouble-free once I worked out how to switch off the annoying transatlantic accented woman's voice: "Hey there! Ah'm here ta help y'all get familiah with yore new computah...".

And I'm typing tonight's diary on the new computah, in the hope that I'll be able to publish it successfully. If you're reading this, you'll know that I've succeeded and if you're not, well yeh'll nevah know what y'all missed.

Popmaster score: Round 1 – 15 points Round 2 – 6 points.

98

～

**Social Distancing Diary – Day 95, a day of cleaning up
computer files. And wheelie bins.**

Today is Thursday June 18, a beautiful morning and a nice
dry walk for a change. And uneventful, apart from having to
get off the road to allow the bin lorry to pass. This particular
road is a single track one, quite common in the more remote
parts of the highlands, and it's wide enough for me, or for the
bin lorry, but not for both of us. And since he's considerably
larger than I am, I'm happy to get out of the way. And there's
always a danger that the bin lifting mechanism might grab me as
it passes, and deposit me unceremoniously into the back of the
truck, amongst the paper and plastic waste. Wouldn't that be a
surprise for the guys down at the recycling centre? "Hey Jimmy,
what should I do with this? It's too heavy to be plastic and too
fat to be paper..."

So you'll have gathered that it's bin day today, this week it
was the turn of the garden refuse and paper/plastic bins to be
emptied. By the time I got back from my morning walk the

paper one had already been cleared and the garden lorry came shortly afterwards. And because I hadn't done it for a long time I decided to clean out both bins before I start refilling them. So it was out with the garden hose and a long handled brush, and they got a good clean out, then left on their sides to dry in the middle of the lawn. Which was a big surprise for El Gato when he jumped over the fence expecting a soft landing.

~~In the hour or so after breakfast and before Popmaster I brought my ECDL skills into play and transferred my files from the old laptop onto the new one. Quite an easy process, and it was a good chance to weed out lots of old unwanted files. I've put all my holiday photos over the years on to a collection of removable drives for ease of portability, so that I can show them to anyone who's interested. Or not interested. If I ever visit you I'll be able to bore entertain you by producing a data stick from my back pocket and talking you through several hundred photos of every railway station, airport and duty free shop I've visited since the turn of the century.~~

I did a wee pruning job today. I could see El Gato looking nervous as I brought the secateurs out from the shed, but he needn't have worried, I'm not going into the veterinary business. Yet.

A stray branch of the dreaded berberis was growing horizontally in the wrong direction so it had to go. But that was all the pruning the berberis got, because, although I hate it, the sparrows love it. It's a safe place for them to take cover from enemies and predators because no sparrowhawk, or indeed cat, would face entering such a spiky environment.

Not that El Gato would bother anyway. One remarkable thing about him is that, although he's constantly hungry and looking out for food, he doesn't pay any attention to the birds. It's quite common to see him sitting on the garden path gazing hopefully at the back door whilst sparrows, blackbirds and noisy starlings are all hopping around within a couple of feet. He thinks that his nourishment comes wrapped in plastic, not feathers.

I've planted out the remaining tomato plants, a very healthy tigerella grown by M from seed and two spindly shirleys bought as plants (and almost killed) by me. There's no room for them in the greenhouse so I've taken a chance and popped them into a large window box outdoors, against a south facing wall. In theory it's quite far north for tomatoes to grow outdoors, but my lovely Italian neighbour has successfully grown them at the back of her house in previous years so maybe I'll have the same success. And I can always pop round for advice. And there's always the chance of a scone. Mamma mia! There goes the diet.

Popmaster score: Round 1 – 6 points Round 2 – 12 points.

99

～

Social Distancing Diary – Day 96, a day of crow trouble. And a bottle of beer.

Today is Friday June 19, dull and misty in the morning and the sun never broke through all day. I still managed the morning walk without a jacket or hat, and a shorter one after lunch. My daily step count seems to have settled around seventeen to nineteen thousand, eight to nine miles. And it's paying off, because this week I've lost another pound. That's eight pounds in six weeks, so I'm almost at my target weight. When I eventually get back into school for a visit no-one will recognise me. I'll probably be ordered to line up with the other little kids. And wear my uniform.

But whilst I'm enjoying the walking, I'm not enjoying the dieting very much. Avoiding snacking is a real test of willpower, especially when M is at work all day. Breakfast used to be cereal and toast, now it's cereal OR toast. Lunch used to be soup, a sandwich, a yoghurt and at least one chocolate biscuit, followed by a snooze. Lunch nowadays is just a sandwich with a healthy filling, a yoghurt and is followed by a walk instead of a snooze. And my daily bottle of beer has become a weekend treat. The good news is that the weekend starts on a Friday. Today it started at 4:14pm.

I cut the grass today. I should have done it yesterday when the sun was shining, but I was assured by the BBC weather channel that today was going to be glorious so I delayed it until today. That was a mistake because it was slightly damp, but I cut it anyway. The only concession I made was that I collected the trimmings rather than leave them lying, because wet grass clippings have a nasty habit of creeping into the house, rather like a certain cat we all know. And since it was I who did the hoovering yesterday I was keen to keep the house clean, at least until it's M's turn to do it.

In other garden news, I got down on my knees and weeded by hand underneath the cypress hedge, which was a mess of long grass and ground elder, and out of reach of the mower. It's also a mess in other ways, because it's an area regularly, erm, "frequented" by the birds. Therefore gloves are compulsory, unless you want your lunchtime sandwich to have a little extra "flavour".

Speaking of birds, Percy the persistent crow has surprised us by appearing with a small companion, whom we suspect is one of his offspring. And Percy Junior, for that is his name, is just as persistent as his father but an awful lot noisier. Constantly cawing, in a croaky high-pitched voice, we always know when he's in the garden. He hasn't yet learned that if he keeps quiet he might get off with staying longer before we realise he's there and chase him. And one of them, or maybe both, has once again broken the peanut feeder, which is designed for small birds, not big heavy ones . The crows seem to take delight in swinging madly on it, like excited kids enjoying a thrilling fairground ride. If it would stop them from wrecking my peanut feeders I'd gladly pay their fare to Disneyland.

When I was feeding El Gato at lunchtime I noticed the feeder lying in pieces, and peanuts scattered all around. I've fixed it many times but it's now beyond help so it's gone in the bin. I've resurrected an old plastic one which I found in M's shed so at least the wee birds can still get access to their peanuts, but it's not as robust as the other one, so I've been keeping a close watch all day to ensure Percy and his boy keep off it. I see them sitting in their tree, watching me, and waiting for a chance to pounce as soon as I turn my back. I can imagine their conversation - Percy to Percy Junior: "Don't worry son, we'll get down there soon. At his age he can't go long without a toilet break".

Popmaster score: Round 1 – 12 points Round 2 – 18 points.

100

Social Distancing Diary – Day 97, a day of Mòd memories

Today is Saturday June 20, and after a very pleasant walk with M I settled down with the papers while she went to Dingwall for the weekly shopping. Supermarkets are still only allowing one person per trolley so I can't go and help, which is maybe just as well because I'm still feeling very nervous about being out amongst people. In fact I have to confess that I couldn't even face going to the post office to return the old BT broadband hub, I had to ask M to do that for me. I'll need to start getting out and about more, though, now that lockdown restrictions are beginning to ease. Mustn't run the risk of being labelled as a hermit. Although M says I am a little crabby at times.

When M came home she announced: "I've brought you a present!" Ooh, excitement – could it be a Birds trifle, a special bottle of beer, or even (sigh) a dream ring? No, it turned out to be a tube of moisturiser which she says will protect my skin from sun damage during my walks. Very thoughtful of her, and I was touched by her concern, but when I read the label closely I spotted the words "anti-ageing". I think she's trying to tell me something but realistically I think she's at least twenty years too late.

Far from being a hermit, today I should have been at the Inverness Provincial Mòd. For those who don't know, in addition to the Royal National Mòd there are a series of provincial, or local, Mòds which are smaller scale versions of the main one which runs in October. They have pretty much the same competitions as the national Mòd, and are a good chance for competitors and choirs to give their songs an airing in a smaller venue and get an adjudication so that they can polish up their performance in preparation for the big event. In my case an awful lot of polish - and elbow grease - was always required.

It's a few years since I last took part in Gaelic singing competitions, but I used to compete at national and local Mòds. With mixed success, to put it kindly. The local Mòds were best for me because there were often very few entrants in the adult competitions and even if I was a sole competitor the local paper would still report: "Gaelic Traditional Singing, Adults – 1st Sandy Thomson, Dingwall". As I basked in this glory, did I confess to my fans that there hadn't been anyone else in the competition? Well, what do you think?

On one occasion, by some miracle, I actually won a senior solo competition at a National Mòd. It was more than twenty years ago, before computers were used to count up scores and I can only imagine the reason I won was that the adjudicator added up the figures wrongly, or put the decimal point in the wrong place.

I got a silver cup to keep for a year, a small cash prize and a spot in that evening's BBC Mòd television programme. The programme was broadcast entirely in Gaelic, and carried subtitles for non-Gaelic viewers, and when I came on my name was shown in Gaelic at the bottom of the screen. Unfortunately, whoever was responsible for the translations that night must have been a little confused because my name was displayed as "Sanndra" instead of "Sandaidh" which, in English, meant that viewers were watching "Sandra" rather than "Sandy". It took me many years of being greeted as "Hi, Sandra" to live that down.

In other news, now that all my files are safely transferred on to the new laptop, the old one has been consigned to the spare room. I'm not going to recycle it just yet, in case a few weeks down the line I discover that there's some vital information I've left on there. Although most of my personal data is stored in my head, there are some things I have difficulty remembering. Bank account details? Memorised years ago. Army number? Engraved on my brain. Wedding anniversary? Erm, let me just check the computer...

101

~∾~

Social Distancing Diary – Day 98, a day of long daylight

Today is Sunday June 21, the so-called "longest day of the year". Well t least that's what it is in the northern hemisphere, I expect it's the shortest day in Wagga Wagga. Of course the day is still twenty-four hours duration, it's the daylight which is at its longest. Here in the north of Scotland it hardly ever gets dark, and further north, in Scandinavia or Iceland, it never gets dark at all. Must be very difficult being a burglar north of the Arctic Circle, I suppose they have to burgle twice as much during the dark winter nights to make up for it.

It was wet this morning but we had our usual long walk before breakfast. Because no-one else is keen, or stupid, enough to go out in the rain we only met one jogger and one car driver. And by lunchtime it had brightened up considerably, with a fresh wind. So fresh, in fact, that I had to reinforce the gazebo's ground pegs and open up its side panels, to stop it from migrating into next door's garden like a big green albatross blown off course.

Today is Father's Day in the UK. All over the country I expect fathers have been awakened early from their Sunday morning long lie by enthusiastic offspring bursting into the bedroom and bouncing on the bed. And the really lucky ones will have had their breakfast cooked and served to them in bed. Nursing a Sunday morning hangover? Sorry but you just have to grin and bear it, we've all been there.

We're long past that stage, however, but thanks to the wonders of technology M Junior arranged for me to receive a personalised Moonpig card from herself and Dog F. Sadly from 120 miles away breakfast in bed wasn't possible so I treated myself to an extra large one of cereal AND toast. I don't think it should affect the weight loss programme, because by bedtime last night I found I had covered more than twenty-two thousand steps yesterday. That was excessive, even for me, so this afternoon I stayed home with a father's day beer while M walked all the way into Dingwall to post my crossword competition entry.

I forgot to tell you – I've started entering "The Times 2" crossword competition on a Saturday. It's a jumbo sized one, with more than a hundred clues, and you can opt to answer the cryptic clues or the easier ones. You can guess which ones I choose. The standard sized cryptic one takes me two or three days to complete, so I'd never get the jumbo one finished in time. As I write this I'm looking at yesterday's standard one, and out of forty clues I've so far solved eleven. That's around one every three hours.

Inside M's Sunday paper today there's a catalogue of garden and household stuff, and she was attracted to a couple of the items advertised. One was a set of garden secateurs and the other was much more exotic – a pack of lion dung. Yes, really. The point of it, as you might guess, is to stop El Gato polluting the garden. After I had fenced off my vegetable plot he simply moved along the path into her flower garden, and we're hoping that a liberal sprinkling of this fragrant product will fool him into thinking we've adopted a lion, and encourage him to find another toilet area. It would certainly work for me.

I wonder where they get the stuff from, does some junior employee have to go out into the African bush at great personal risk, armed only with a shovel? Or do they have some sort of supply contract with Edinburgh Zoo, whereby the lions are trained to do their erm, "business", into a 500g cardboard box?

And I wonder if it will still be warm when it arrives.

102

~

Social Distancing Diary – Day 99, a day of recycling

Today is Monday June 22, M was back at work so I had the morning walk on my own. It was mild and dry when I set off so I didn't bother with a jacket or hat. Just as I reached the stables on the way home, with just over a mile to go, the rain came on. There's an open fronted tractor shed at the stables, so I took shelter just inside to give me a chance to assess how heavy the rain was going to be. But after a few minutes I thought I should move on in case the owners spotted me and suspected me of planning to steal their tractor. If it had been a John Deere I might have been tempted, but it's a Massey Ferguson so no self respecting tractor thief is going to steal that. As Farmer J says: "If it's red, leave it in the shed".

Anyway, the rain didn't get too heavy and half an hour later I was home having a warm shower while the wet clothes were in the tumble dryer. And until my walking clothes were dry I took the chance to dress smartly for a change, which was a real boost to my self confidence. So much so that after Popmaster I drove to Dingwall and in an act of great bravery visited the recycling centre. I had quite a few small electrical items for recycling, some of which have been sitting forlornly in the shed for a long time. So I waved them all goodbye as they disappeared into the appropriate container. A special farewell was reserved for the hated Dyson, as it was despatched off to Hoover Heaven. Or maybe Hoover Hell. It certainly made my life hell for the past ten years.

Actually, what happens to the small electrical items is that they're collected by a company who either refurbish them or break them up for parts. So there's a good chance the Dyson will get a clean up and a service, and end up with a new family. I wish them luck. It will be like taking on a new puppy, all lovely and cuddly at first but after a day or two they'll realise it's impossible to train.

After the recycling centre visit I took a walk along Dingwall High Street, just to see how it felt, and it was much less scary than the last time I did it. There were very few people around and of course most of the shops are still closed. Including Harry Gows, which is only open Tuesday to Saturday. I wonder whether I can invent an excuse to go to town again tomorrow?

I drove home the long way round. Up the Ullapool road to Marybank and across to Muir of Ord, passing the distillery. Which is another source of temptation. Glen Ord whisky and Harry Gow's dream rings – I'm surrounded by temptations.

By the time I got home my scruffy clothes were dry so I got changed and got stuck into some serious gardening. There's a border that runs alongside the new fence which has a variety of shrubs and bushes growing, including the dreaded berberis. It has been pretty messy for a few years now, with a wooden edging which is now rotten and unsightly, so my mission over the next few days is to sort it out. The border is around eleven metres in length so if I do a couple of metres a day I'll be able to stretch the job out for the week and on Friday I can say "Phew what a busy week I've had, I deserve a beer".

In the afternoon I did the long walk again, in the opposite direction. That brought my step count up to more than twenty-six thousand today. I hope that will cancel out all the calories from the weekend's beer.

Popmaster score: Round 1 – 9 points Round 2 – 6 points.

103

⌇

Social Distancing Diary – Day 100, a day of history lessons. And tangles.

Today is Tuesday June 23. A hundred days, eh? Imagine that! Such a lot can happen in a hundred days, and a quick history lesson reveals a couple of interesting 100-day periods. Firstly, the Hundred Days War, which ran from 20 March to 8 July 1815, a total of 111 days. Which just goes to show that Napoleon might have been a great leader but he'd never have passed O'Grade Arithmetic.

And later, in 1933, US President Franklin Roosevelt's "100 days" refers to the period when he successfully introduced measures to end the great depression and set America back on its feet. And as a bonus he began to end prohibition and made it legal to sell beer and wine. That's my kind of president.

Once again, I'm a winner! On Day Five I won a prize in the Scottish Children's Lottery, and ninety-five days later I've done it again. Back then my prize was a free entry into the next week's draw and guess what? I didn't win. This time it's the same again, another free entry for Thursday's draw. Surely I'll win this time? Come on Children's Lottery, stop teasing me.

On Popmaster today it was nice to hear a contestant from Perth. That's Perth, Scotland, by the way, in case my Australian readers get over-excited. Perth is a beautiful city, but it hardly ever gets a mention on national media. Overshadowed by Glasgow and Edinburgh, Perth is a place on a signpost that you see as you pass by on your way north, to Dingwall.

Anyway, I felt sorry for the girl on Popmaster, she got the most horrifically hard questions, and I got the same ones correct as she did, with one extra. And that was only because I'm old enough to remember 1973. And Suzi Quatro. Who, by the way - for younger readers - was an American rock star, not a 4x4 sports utility vehicle.

Postie brought me a letter today, from my new BFF Nicola, thanking me for helping to tackle the Covid-19 crisis. Wasn't that nice of her? She says that we have made great progress together, she and I, and that's why she is writing to me now. I must say I feel very honoured that Nicola has singled me out for this praise but I feel sure that some of the rest of you have probably done something too. Anyway, when the knighthood comes around I'll be happy to accept it on your behalf.

It was dry and warm in the afternoon, so I cut the grass. First though, I had to trim the edges using the petrol strimmer and it was all going well until, all of a sudden, the Twang of Doom! For those of you not familiar with the finer points of grass strimming, the Twang of Doom is the sound of the nylon cord running out and the final couple of inches being cast out of the strimmer at a hundred miles an hour, like some sort of high-speed fluorescent worm.

Of course it always happens at the most awkward time, just when you're halfway through and got yourself into a good rhythm, and you have to interrupt the job and install new nylon. And of course it's a year since you last did it and you can't remember how on earth the strimmer head comes apart and once you work that out there's always a wee spring that, well, springs out and loses itself in the grass. And once you overcome all these challenges you find that as soon as you take your roll of nylon out of its container it immediately ties itself into impossible tangles and you need three hands to get the blasted stuff wrapped around the reel.

Who was it that said gardening was a relaxing hobby?

Popmaster score: Round 1 – 9 points Round 2 – 9 points.

104

～

Social Distancing Diary – Day 101, a day of looking back. And forward.

Today is Wednesday June 25, and the heatwave which was forecast seemed to have bypassed us. The morning dawned dull and damp but I got almost all the way round my morning walk before I needed to open my umbrella. After I got home, though, it began to rain persistently so my plan of clearing another two metres of shrub border had to be abandoned. And by the time the rain stopped it was lunchtime, and then the promised heatwave arrived. Oh dear, it was rather hot for working outside so little progress was made, and I was relieved when M came home and gave me an excuse to stop. And when she presented me with a choc ice that was the end of work for the day.

The wet morning was spent indoors with Popmaster and the papers. Luckily Wednesday is one of the days when M buys me The Times, so that gave me a good hour's worth of reading. And the crosswords give me many hours of mental exercise too. There are two of them, a "quick cryptic" which I can usually crack in one sitting, and the "real" Times Crossword which is legendarily difficult and takes me several days. And I usually need Mr Google's help with it.

Early in 2019 I had a touch of "old man's trouble" and had to have a routine operation. Although the op was very minor there was a long recovery period at home, during which I wasn't allowed to drive, to lift anything or do anything strenuous. Anyway, to help pass the time during this period, which was around three to four weeks, I bought a book of 100 Times quick cryptic crosswords. And I was up and about and back to my normal active self long before I got anywhere near number 100.

Incidentally, I think that was when I began to pile on the pounds which I'm now trying desperately to lose. A combination of inactivity and boredom is very dangerous if your willpower is as pathetic as mine. Added to that was the fact that M, being her typical caring self, often used to come home from work with treats for me. And some of them were ring-shaped and dreamy.

A hundred and one days ago when I started this diary, lockdown was still some time away and we were hoping it wouldn't happen. But I had plans in case it did happen. I fully intended to improve my Gaelic, improve my guitar playing, learn some new songs and maybe even pick up my watercolour painting after a gap of several years. And how have all these plans panned out? Gaelic = no change. Guitar playing = worse than ever. Songs learnt = none. Paintings completed = nil.

Now as some of you will know, this will be the last Social Distance Diary for the time being. I'm quite amazed by how many of you have become fans and followers, and I enjoy very much your comments. My life is very ordinary, uneventful, some might say boring, and I can't believe how it can attract so much interest. And because every day is as mundane as the previous one, a hundred and one consecutive days of trying to find humour in everyday situations has been very challenging. And doing Popmaster every day is pretty hard going too, as my poor record shows.

I'm going to have a break for a few weeks for some exciting family time and then I hope to resume writing, but it won't be on a daily basis. In the meantime please stay safe and well, and do keep in touch, it's always nice to hear from you. And watch this space, there might, just might, be a book on the horizon.

Popmaster score: Round 1 – 6 points Round 2 – 9 points.

Finally, I leave you with these wise words from that most scholarly of bears, Winnie the Pooh:

"I think we dream so we don't have to be apart for so long. If we're in each other's dreams, we can be together all the time"

Mind you, he also said: "I wasn't going to eat it, I was just going to taste it"

105

⌒

Social Distancing Diary – Day 114, a day of welcoming a new arrival

Today is Wednesday July 8, and this is a special diary entry.

Yesterday was a day of firsts. It was the first time in three months that I've been dressed up in proper clothes, the first time I've worn a wristwatch, the first time I've driven more than a couple of miles, and the first time M and I have been able to meet a very special person.

Regular readers will remember M Junior and her bump, who featured regularly in diary entries. Well now there's another personality to tell you about, because bump has disappeared, and Alice Mary Smith has arrived.

Alice was born in Ninewells Hospital, Dundee, early on Thursday July 2 and is the pride and joy of her parents Farmer J and M Junior, and little sister to Dog F.

And gorgeous first granddaughter to M and me, who are both absolutely besotted.

Many of you have heard this news already, and thank you for

your comments and kind wishes. I expect to come back down to earth in a few weeks, and hope to resume regular diaries sometime after then.

In the meantime please excuse me while I look at the photos of Alice one more time.......

Thank you so much for buying my book, I hope you've enjoyed sharing my social distancing experiences.

I'm always happy to hear your comments and thoughts, you can reach me by email at sandy_thomson3@hotmail.co.uk